THE DEER HUNTER'S OATH

Kay,
Only someone from
the "Basin" would
understand some of
this book
Jeff

JEFF LINDSTROM

ISBN-13: 978-1508595823
ISBN-10: 1508595828

Edited by Erin Brisk

PREFACE

While riding with my wife across my old stomping grounds and regaling her with deer hunting exploits of old, she mentioned that I should write them down for our now 14 grandsons. I am not a real writer and have never pretended to be so. The only way I got through college was to have my dear wife correct the grammar and punctuation on my papers and then type them. I still don't type well, so this process has been a bit painful.

This book is 97.3 percent factual, but as in all hunting and fishing stories some liberties have been taken. Indeed, I think that the stories told are well above average in their credibility. Some names (but not near enough) have been changed to protect the guilty or stupid. As with most endeavors, if you hunt long enough you will initiate or participate in an action that you hope no one will ever include in a book.

I hope you enjoy this small slice of the people and experiences that have blessed my life.

Note: I am a member of The Church of Jesus Christ of Latter Day Saints , or "Mormons", so if you find an ecclesiastical or lifestyle reference that confuses you please go to **https://www.lds.org** for more insight.

ACKNOWLEDGMENTS

To my brothers Larry, Grant, Gordon, and Craig for correcting my faulty memories.

To my sister Cindy for living with five brothers.

To Mom and Dad for raising me.

To the Monday Lunch Brain Trust: Brad, Clyde, Dave, Jeff, and Jim for the encouragement.

Most of all to my dear wife Lynne for absolutely everything

CONTENTS

CHAPTER I

THE DEER HUNTER'S OATH

There are defining moments in a young man's life: his first car, his first kiss, and probably most important in our family.......his first deer hunt. There were rules and tradition that must be observed. Rule number one was that deer camp was open only to men, no women allowed! I am not sure whether this rule originated with the men or the women. Although she would certainly be lonely, I think my wife secretly looked forward to me taking the six boys hunting. If we did not come home in a reasonable time, (say two months), I am sure she would have had someone start looking for us.

Rule number two was that you had to be eight years old to go on the hunt. This seemed logical because at this age most boys are out of diapers and can keep up with dad on the hikes. If you listen carefully on the Friday before the third Saturday in October, you can hear the plaintive wail of six- and seven-year-old males that are watching their dads and brothers drive away with rifles and camping gear. I know this is true because I once was one.

A side note here on the relative ranking of events in an eight year olds life. It is rumored that a Lindstrom boy, upon being interviewed by the Bishop for his upcoming baptism, was asked the silly question, "What happens when you turn eight years old?" His first response was, "I get to go deer hunting," followed closely by, "and I get a hunting knife." I am not sure where "Baptism" came in, but I hope it was somewhere in the top ten.

The two life events that were constantly jockeying for position of importance were Christmas and deer hunting. One year Christmas might edge out the deer hunt, but another year it could easily reverse. Either way, the dates were close enough together to make it a glorious season of the year.

After years, and years, and years, the magical moment finally arrives. You are eight years old and it is the Friday before the opening of the deer hunt. You probably slept very little

Thursday night in anticipation. You go to school and a small miracle occurs. Your dad shows up at about 11:30 to rescue you. There are few sweeter experiences that leaving school early and laughing at the poor schmucks whose dads don't love them enough to take them deer hunting.

From the school you are taken to the shop. The shop was the location of Lindstrom Brothers Heating, owned by my Dad, Uncle Bert, and Uncle Charlie. Here, final preparations are being made for the journey. An old five gallon galvanized milk can that Uncle Charlie soldered a tap into is used for drinking water. A sheet metal ice chest that was previously fabricated in the shop is filled with food and loaded into the bed of the truck. A folding camp table that assembles like a jigsaw puzzle is also loaded at this time. It is of ingenious design, undoubtedly taken from detailed plans from a past issue of Popular Mechanics.

A checklist is counted out loud: License - check, rifle - check, ammo - check, sleeping bag - check, etc. The list is in order of importance for a successful hunt. One year Cousin Brian forgot to check off item number four when he forgot his sleeping bag and had to endure a long, cold night. It wouldn't have been so bad if he had not completed his annual fall-in-the-creek routine. Brian fell in the creek every year but one until he was sixteen. The year he did not fall in the creek, we had changed camp locations to the mountain behind the ranch house. With the creek not within reasonable walking distance, he had to be content with tripping and falling into a sizeable mud hole.

The trucks that would carry us to the happy hunting grounds were lowly work trucks the rest of the year. They were regular cab, long bed, half ton pickups. Extended, club, super, double, and crew cabs were still in the design stage of Detroit's automobile engineers. We were mainly Ford men with the exception of Uncle Bert, who once had a '66 Chevy. Later on we did have some Dodges that were bought at a government auction of surplus vehicles, but I would rather forget them. By the way, when you go to the temple you will see very few Dodge pickups in the parking lot. This is because it is a well known fact that Dodge owners lie about their gas mileage, thereby making them unable to get a temple recommend. I have never met someone that drove a Dodge that didn't claim to get at least 24 miles per gallon (especially the diesels).

All of the trucks we had were two wheel drive. In the 60's it was a rarity to see a 4X4 pickup. Your truck was considered off-road worthy if a set of tire chains resided in the bed.

With the gear loaded in the trucks it was time to get the intrepid hunters situated. Seating was always a seniority-driven affair. The older you were the better chance you had of riding in the front. Once the three oldest men were ensconced in the cab, the younger men and boys piled in the bed with the camping gear. This was exciting until about age sixteen; after that you dreamed of owning your own hunting jeep.

We stopped for gas on the way out of town, and if we whined enough Dad would buy us an orange soda or my personal favorite, grape Nehi.

I remember thinking that we had gone quite a distance when we reached the mouth of Provo Canyon (which was maybe ten miles). Our route then took us past Spring Glen, Bridal Veil Falls, Upper Falls, Wildwood, and onto Deer Creek Dam. If you were a prepared young man, you had a couple of marbles or rocks ready when approaching the Dam. As we slowed for the curve we all moved to the right side of the truck to see if we could throw our object of choice into the spillway and envision it going all the way to the pool at the bottom.

After the reservoir, we usually turned at the sawmill before Heber and took the shortcut through Daniels. Next stop was Whiskey Springs. We drank the cold water and pretended it made us drunk. We proceeded up Daniels

Canyon, across Strawberry, and down Deep Creek until we reached the ranch at Fruitland. We turned off highway 40, went down the dugway, crossed the log bridge that dad had made, and camped near Current Creek.

Size and distance are things that change with time. I remember going to Grovecrest Elementary School for parents' night with my two oldest sons, Clint and Ryan. I couldn't believe how the halls had shrunk since I was there in the fifth grade. Likewise, distances seem to shrink with age. When I was eight, I was sure that it took at least six hours to get to the ranch, but it was really only about an hour and a half.

As the truck rolled to a stop at our campsite, the youngsters leapt to the ground and quite often let out a war whoop. I don't know how much testosterone a boy of eight has, but judging by his actions he could join the Marines when he got home. After the long ride and drinking an orange soda or coffee, everyone found a tree to their liking and marked it.

With the preliminaries out of the way, the business of setting up camp was begun. An old white canvas wall tent was erected using screw-together poles that somewhat resembled 3/4" gas line found at the shop. An old stove was installed and a lively debate usually ensued as to whether or not the flue would catch the tent on fire during the night. The agreed solution was usually to let the stove go out before bedtime. The ring of rocks used for the fire had to be rearranged due to the damage done by the cattle during the previous year. Uncle Bert directed some of the younger hunters to scout for firewood, collect it, and report back with their arms loaded. This activity was much anticipated because of the "need" to use a hatchet or axe.

As the older members of the contingent finished setting up camp, the younger ones started exploring. There were rocks and trees to climb, an old shed to explore, and some relics of the previous owner's garbage (treasures), from the last 75 years. After the initial flurry of energy started slowing somewhat, we set down to the serious business of throwing cans and bottles into the creek and trying to hit and sink them before your brother or cousin could. .22 LR shells were like gold then. You saved all year to make sure you had enough for the deer hunt. About the time that ammo was running low Uncle Russ (who we thought had secret military connections), would call us over and hand out a box of 50 to each boy.

After he had outgrown his Daisy BB gun and Benjamin air rifle, the .22 rifle was every boy's dream. Those of us who relate to the gun lust Ralphy exhibited in "A Christmas Story" share a common bond. Yes, if you are as old as I am, that movie is an accurate representation of life at that time.

When I was about ten or eleven I saw my "Red Ryder," but in the form of an Ithaca Model 49 .22 single-shot saddle carbine in the display case of Park's Sportsman Store. Oh how I wanted, no, needed that gun. I left many subtle and not so subtle hints with my Dad. It would feed our family, protect us from burglars, and get me out of the house. For a month or two I would run home from school to check the gun rack in my bedroom to see if my dad or the good fairy had heard my pleas and left the rifle in the spot I had left open for it. Reality arrived before the Ithaca did so I moved on to other dreams.

Dad promised me a .22 if I earned my Eagle Scout Rank. By the time I earned it, my desires had moved on to a Winchester semi auto model 290. When I was about 12, Dad allowed me to carry my .22 as we hiked and hunted deer. I had visions of finishing off dad's mortally wounded deer or supplying the camp with fresh rabbit and grouse, but mainly I learned that a gun without a sling gets heavy.

As the sun started setting over Murphy's ranch, attention was given to starting a fire. Our scout training was now going to be put the test. Usually we were successful, but other times

Uncle Bert told us to stand back as he soaked the logs with white gas, threw a match and ran. I still don't know exactly what white gas consisted of, but you could buy it at Carters Service Station and use it for Coleman stoves, lanterns, and starting fires.

The camp table jigsaw puzzle was assembled so dinner could begin. I have heard of camps where real Dutch oven feasts are prepared, but most of the men in our camp got married because they couldn't cook and were starving to death. Mom cooked a very large roast for the trip the night before, so dinner was self-serve roast beef sandwiches on Wonder Bread, with homemade cookies for dessert.

After dinner was done, preparations for the morning hunt commenced. I was not old enough to have firsthand knowledge of the planning that went into the storming of Iwo Jima, but it probably resembled Friday evening in deer camp. Rifles were cleaned and ammo was checked. The more experienced hunters only carried 10 or 15 cartridges, but the younger hunters were debating on whether to take two or three boxes. There was some wisdom in this since I personally witnessed Cousin Lee quit shooting at a deer because he was foolish enough to carry only one box of 20 shells and ran out.

If you were a man in our camp you shot a 30 caliber rifle. Dad shot a 300 Savage. Uncles Charlie, Russ, Evan, and Grandpa Colledge favored the old standard 30-06. Uncle Bert shot the new up and coming .308. The less serious and younger hunters had to be content with a borrowed 30-30. Uncle Mark showed up one year with a woman's gun (270), and by a close vote was barely allowed to stay in camp. He was told that he would receive no help if he only wounded a deer using a pansy gun.

Along with being allowed to go on the hunt when you were eight, you received your first honest-to-goodness real hunting knife. It was a large, fixed blade in a leather sheath. You needed this to help your dad gut the deer he would shoot tomorrow morning. I was more than a little disappointed when my dad shot a deer and started gutting it with his Old Timer pocket knife. Luckily, I had a real knife to help him finish. A Friday evening ritual was the sharpening of your hunting knife. The various ways and styles of sharpening were discussed and debated. The actual sharpening concluded when you rolled up the sleeve of your hunting shirt and tried shaving your arm to prove your skills.

Proper hunting attire was readied for the morning. This usually consisted of your hunting pants, hunting shirt, hunting boots, and hunting hat, which all strangely resembled your normal play clothes. The one big exception was your new red sweatshirt. Now they call them hoodies, but to us they were just red sweatshirts with a hood and one big pocket in the front. The only purpose I knew the front pocket to serve was to hold your morning hunting supplies, which were an apple, and a candy bar if you were lucky.

Hunter orange had not been invented yet so the approved colors were red and yellow. Dad also brought us a pair of too-big brown jersey hunting gloves which looked somewhat similar to the gloves at the HVAC supply house used for gas piping. We never carried a pack or canteen for that matter. We were too poor to "hydrate," so we just drank lots of water.

With dinner over and darkness setting in, everyone gathered around the campfire. As the youngsters kept the fire alive by poking it every couple of minutes, the men started with the stories. They ranged from growing up in the now ghost town of Mammoth, Utah, to where they had served in World War II, and onto, of course, deer stories. I use the word 'stories' in its purest sense. At one time they were accurate reports of actual events, but as the years went by the deer got bigger, the shots got farther, and the snow got deeper. The youngsters listened in wide-eyed amazement of the skills and apparent humility of the older generation.

When the conversation reached the appropriate time, Uncle Mark would call out the new eight year olds. He was a security guard that did not carry a gun but did have a real badge that he held up for all to see. He would have them form a straight line and bring their right arm to the square. He informed them it was now time for them to recite and commit to the DEER HUNTER'S OATH. As I remember, it went something like this:

ON MY HONOR I PROMISE THAT I WILL NEVER TELL MY MOTHER WHAT HAPPENS AT DEER CAMP.

I WILL NOT TELL HER ABOUT THE DRINKING,

OR THE SMOKING,

OR THE SWEARING,

OR MOST OF ALL,

ABOUT THE DANCING GIRLS THAT WILL SHOW UP FROM TABIONA AFTER DARK.

After this lifelong commitment was made, the new hunter was accepted into the brotherhood with all the associated rights, honors, and privileges.

The campfire was extinguished and when the majority of the men surrounding it agreed that it would not flare up during the night, we retired to the tent. The final act of the night was lying snugly in your sleeping bag and watching the Coleman lantern slowly get dimmer until it was dark and your only concern was how to get to sleep with the biggest day of your life waiting for you in the morning.

THE DEER HUNTER'S OATH

CHAPTER 2

THE MEN OF DEER CAMP

Some people who don't hunt assume that the motivation of those that do is their desire to kill and watch something die. I have never met such a hunter, and if I ever do we will soon part ways. The ability to take a life requires that it be done in the least traumatic way possible. As the years go by my priorities have steadily shifted from making sure that I got my deer no matter what, to making a good clean shot that puts the animal down quickly. This philosophy has been an ongoing process that started when I first shot a sparrow, on through my bird and rabbit days, into the competitive young deer hunter stage, and slowly ending up as an old man that sometimes lets things "get away."

Killing a deer is such a small part of the deer hunting experience. The goals, skills, and motivations of each hunter vary dramatically. Although I often enjoy the solitude of being alone on the mountain, many of my dearest memories are of the relationships developed in a lifetime of deer hunting. I will describe my perception of the men of our deer camp.

Grandpa Colledge: My grandpa, my mother's dad, was a unique individual. It is said that we are all unique, but some are just more unique than others. They didn't have ADHD when he was alive, but if they did, he would qualify, and maybe even have a few extra capital letters to add. I never remember him just sitting. He was tying flies, improving a set of folding camper steps, inventing some novel piece of outdoor equipment, learning calligraphy, or just tinkering.

On the wall in my office I have a picture of him hanging under the deer he shot in the early 60's. It is still the biggest deer any of our party has ever taken. It is a 7X9 that is 30" wide. The picture was taken at about the time he shot the big buck. He was only about 5'6" but had the presence of an army officer. He is shod with a pair of lace up mining boots that stopped just short of his knees. His red top wool hunting socks poke out the top. His wool trousers are of the old cavalry style that ballooned at the thighs and are held up by a belt that he made himself out of leather he probably tanned. On the belt rode his bowie knife, cartridge case, sharpening stone, and sometimes a .22 pistol.

He is wearing the requisite red checkered shirt under a canvas coat covered with pockets that he designed and grandma had sewn. In fact, she made a hunting coat for most of the men in the camp. A pair of 10X50 navy surplus binoculars with a rabbit fur strap hang from his neck. His red hat usually had a longer-than-normal bill to shade his eyes. In his hand is an ex-military Springfield 30-06 that he got from the NRA for $30 and sporterized. It had a custom stock that Uncle Evan helped with.

He is leaning against a military jeep that he refurbished. It had a shovel and axe bolted above the front bumper, was painted bright yellow, and the inscription "Old Yeller" was hand-lettered on body. Even if he never shot a deer, he was quite the sight to behold.

Grandpa orchestrated the opening morning of the hunt somewhat like I imagine the Battle of the Bulge unfolded. He would give his son and sons-in-law their orders. Dad said we had three kinds of sons in our camp; sons, sons-in-law, and sons of bitches.

Grandpa barked, "Dennis, you go to the rock below the low road," "Evan, you push toward the pines," "Darrell, you go to the upper road," and "Paul, you head to the big draw." He informed everyone that there would be a radio check at 09:30 on the ten pound WWII surplus walkie talkies that he was handing out. My dad usually told him to go to hell. He was the only one that regularly stood up to grandpa and, as a result, they had a great relationship. Grandpa's deer hunting "experience" was as much about the "campaign" as actually shooting the deer.

Uncle Bert: He was my dad's older brother, a diabetic and camp cook. His job as camp cook required that he get out the bread and makings for sandwiches that you made yourself. He always had a good natured comment for the younger hunters and a wise crack about the skills of the teenage hunters. To the cousins he was affectionately known as Uncle Bert Baby. He shot a pre-'64 Winchester .308 that is now a collector's item, but back then was just another rifle. He usually got his deer but was not too upset when he didn't. When they were legal, he once shot a doe at the urging of his son and then had to listen to the resulting insults for close to a decade.

Uncle Charlie: He was dad's younger brother and the quiet one. He seldom spoke and spent most of his life trying to quit smoking. The most I ever heard him talk was around the campfire late at night after a bottle and paper cups had been passed out. None of our group were real drinkers, but the night before the hunt seemed to be a moment in time that afforded special liberties.

The campfire talk usually ended with quiet stories about their experiences during the war (WWII). Charlie used a Remington 760 pump in 30-06 that often seemed to jam and not feed well from the clip. He was considered a good shot and I remember him usually getting a three point somewhere near the Strawberry side.

Uncle Mark: He married dad's oldest sister. We considered him a city slicker since he lived in Salt Lake City. He worked at Kennecott in security and would pull out his badge and act official if the need arose. He was the administrator of the "Deer Hunter's Oath" and a favorite of the youngsters. He was quite the high school athlete and often told stories of the "glory days." He had this niche pretty much to himself because the Lindstroms were not gifted in sports and seldom went to high school. He shot a 30-06 and when he later switched to a 270 had to endure the taunts of using a "woman's" gun. I only remember him shooting one deer in the decade he was a part of camp.

When he got to camp on Friday the first thing he did was to change from his city shoes to a pair of green Irish Setter boots. I couldn't figure out how they lasted him 10 years but I think that he only wore them one weekend a year.

Uncle Russ: He married dad's middle sister and was military from his crew cut to his aviator glasses. He had flown in WWII and stayed in or close to the Air Force until he retired.

He had a nice camper that kids were not allowed in. He of course shot a 30-06 and had the first of any hunt-related paraphernalia. He had the first 3x9 variable scope that I ever saw and was reputed to reload his own ammo. He had all the equipment but he never shot a deer that I knew of. He was observed missing a deer one time and when he got back to camp complained that his scope must be off. My Dad grabbed his rifle and had a kid run across the creek to set a Coors bottle on the hill at about 100 yards. Dad leaned over the hood of the Ford and squeezed of a shot. The bottle exploded, Dad handed Russ back his gun and stated, "That's the problem, the scope is off." I don't think Russ knew how to handle our side of the family but tried his best and was always good for a box of .22 shells for us kids.

Uncles Daryl, Dennis, and Evan were from Mom's side of the family and usually had enough sense to avoid our camp, but one year stands out. Evan, Cousin Neal, and Cousins-in-Law Gary and Rob showed up for the evening hunt. It was a beautiful warm fall day and we did see a few deer. They decided to go home, re-gear and come back for the morning hunt. I was staying on the river in an old camper that we placed on the ground for the season.

In the morning I woke up and tried to open the door but it was stuck. I pushed hard, moved a snow drift and stepped into a winter wonderland (nightmare). It had snowed almost a foot during the night. With the wind howling I thought for sure that they would not make it for the morning hunt.

Just as it was getting light they pulled up in Grandpa's jeep, Old Yeller. We churned up the mountain and spent most of the morning getting unstuck. We had given up and were heading down the mountain when a deer was spotted running below us. It was almost out of range but some in the party felt it necessary to shoot at the snow near its feet to send it on its way.

Occasionally some of Dad's friends showed up in camp. The Fowles boys were always welcome. Don was Dad's best friend in school and always was quick with a joke or to whip out his volunteer police badge if trespassers were encountered. Grant was a short, tough man who could out hike everyone well into his 70's. If you were ever in a tight spot he is someone you would want to come help. He was 50 years ahead of his time since his hair was one big wiry cowlick that went every direction at once. A little gel and he would fit right in today.

Dad (Paul, JP): Dad was the de facto leader of the camp, mainly because we lived on the ranch at one time and he knew the mountains and locals. When I was eight, I remember following behind dad and hiking at least ten miles (well maybe one mile). I thought I was being quiet like he taught me, but after taking my six sons on their inaugural hunt it is a wonder that we even got close to a deer. Somehow we did get close enough and Dad shot a spike. He showed me how to use my new hunting knife and we returned to camp triumphant.

Dad was patient with all five of us boys and was more interested in being a Dad than a hunter. Grandpa would see us back at camp and say, "Paul, I could hear you and your boys clear across the canyon." Dad would reply, "Maybe, but I get as many deer as you do."

Dad always drove the truck, hauled out the deer and made sure everyone got back to camp. He helped anyone get a deer if they were serious about it, and yet always seemed to get his own in the process.

He was one of the best rifle shots I have ever seen. When he was in his 70's we took him up the mountain and found a three point on the oak brush side hill. It was at least 250 yards so I got my 257 Weatherby and was ready to shoot when Dad missed, or finish it off if he was lucky enough to wound it. His 300 Savage spoke and the deer dropped in its tracks. Dad was interested in deer hunting, but was serious about having a family experience.

Most normal families have a reunion at the park, but at least once a year ours was held at deer camp. The outdoors provided a venue unlike any other for learning about what really makes a person tick. When you hike, camp, cook, joke, get stuck, get lost, get frustrated, and get mentored, it's hard not to become part of the people you are with. The relationships with those involved become more meaningful and lasting. In the last 50 years a lot of my best memories come from the experiences I had with the men of deer camp.

CHAPTER 3

FRUITLAND

Many of my early deer related experiences happened on, or around, our ranch near Fruitland, Utah. Fruitland isn't really a town, or even a wide spot in the road. It was originally called Rabbit Gulch, but land developers started calling it Fruitland in 1907. They hoped the name change might make it easier to sell the farmland. The ground might grow some crops, but fruit was not one of them.

Fruitland is marked by a very small white church that was occasionally occupied. A mile to the west was the Current Creek Lodge and gas station; a mile to the east was a general store. There was a small collection of ranches within about a five mile radius. This was the closest thing to civilization for 30 miles, although "civilized" would not be an adjective that would first come to mind when describing the residents of that locale. I am not sure how we ended up there but the following is my best guess.

Dad grew up in the now ghost town of Mammoth, Utah, which was still a rough, tough, desolate place in the 20's and 30's. The only thing that grew was sagebrush, and even it struggled. He and his brother Bert were enterprising young men and started raising a few chickens in their backyard. This may have sparked his desire to be a rancher, because he would have been happy living in the 1800's on a cattle ranch.

After he got home from WWII, his ranching dreams took a backseat to construction and eventually being an ironworker. He traveled the Western United States for five years but never had a job located in his home county. He and his brothers, Bert and Charlie, started Lindstrom Brothers Heating in 1953 so they could work closer to home.

In 1960 an opportunity arose to purchase a ranch on Current Creek in Fruitland, Utah. Dad volunteered to manage the ranch while the brothers kept the HVAC company running. The ranch was comprised of an old log home, outbuildings, some cattle, sheep, and about 1,000 acres, of which 80 were in alfalfa.

Our family moved to the ranch in the spring of 1961. I was eight years old and as excited as if Christmas and the opening of deer hunting were rolled into one. The directions to our place included the phrase "and then you turn off the paved road," and not by just a little ways. About half a mile off Highway 40 the road went down a steep, twisting dugway that hugged the hill and ended at the rickety bridge over Current Creek (or, as the locals call it, Kern Krik). To this day I can still place someone that grew up in the "basin" by the twang in their speech.

I think that Mom refused to ride in the truck across the dilapidated bridge so the SECOND improvement to the ranch was a stronger bridge. Dad cut some Doug Fir on the mountain and dragged them to the river with the D4 Cat to build a *newer* rickety bridge.

Once the creek was crossed, it was a short jaunt to the ranch house. I was too young to have understood the look on Mom's face when she first laid eyes on the 'house," but can imagine that Dad had some serious explaining to do. The old house was built of squared logs, had a large kitchen/gathering area and two bedrooms. The outhouse was fifty feet to the east, which was way too close to the house. Even with the prevailing westerly breeze, one whiff could turn your stomach. At a very young age I could have qualified to free dive for pearls as I learned how to hold my breath for up to 3 minutes. The first time I looked down the hole, I thought it rivaled the stalagmite formations in Timpanogos Cave.

The outhouse was a nice two-seater (but to this day I am curious as to why I would want to share that intimate moment), which brings us to the FIRST ranch improvement, an inside bathroom. Once the cesspool was complete and the toilet installed, Dad dumped five gallons of diesel fuel in the outhouse and lit a match. I don't think the initial flare up was from the fuel, but when it did catch fire it was a beautiful sight. I also finally understood why the pioneers used buffalo chips. They really do burn.

With all summer lying before us, I could see that living here would be almost as fun as deer hunting and camping in a tent.

The house had two bedrooms but our family had four kids, so Larry and I set up army cots with sleeping bags in the wraparound screened porch that was on two sides of the cabin (I mean house). We were not deer hunting and camping in a tent, but when the summer rains fell on the metal roof over the porch and we were snug in our bags, we were content.

When we determined that Mom had the house under control, Larry and I accepted the serious responsibility of exploration. We started with the spring that supplied our drinking water. It bubbled up through the sand so we determined that it was indeed "quicksand." Several hours were spent trying to "find the bottom" with long sticks. Surrounding the spring was a swamp that held numerous varieties of frogs, snakes, and dragonflies. They were great entertainment, but when we discovered leeches on our legs it was time we moved on to dry ground.

Now that we were soaking wet it was off to the barns. There was a large barn with a rail and pulley system near the top used to stack hay. Considerable thought went into figuring a way to make a roller coaster ride out of it, but sadly that dream died.

On the north side of the barn was the tack shed. By climbing on the top of it, we were only about eight feet below a little crow's nest area that was at the peak of the barn. A hole about two feet square opened to a little shelf on the inside of the barn. I told Larry that since he was such a good climber, he could hold on to the edge of the roof and pull himself up the steep barn roof. I explained that once he was at the top he could swing a leg over and sit in the crow's nest. Wouldn't that be cool?

I never thought he would actually do it, but he did, and his excitement turned to utter panic as he looked down 25 feet to the barn floor and realized he couldn't get down. I had to go get dad and we talked him into lowering himself over the edge so Dad could catch him. I explained that I had no clue why anybody would be dumb enough to climb up there.

The small shed that housed the old Ford tractor held little interest for us, so it was off to the large equipment shed. A large John Deere tractor resided there along with the bailer, mower, rake, and a half century's worth of miscellaneous parts and pieces of farm equipment. The west end of the large shed was enclosed for a workshop which was a veritable treasure trove of ancient tools, bolts, and a few things we could not explain.

One of the unknown items was about a quarter of an inch in diameter, brass, and a couple of inches long. We thought we had discovered some strange type of rifle cartridge but when Dad identified them as blasting caps our exploration parameters were somewhat adjusted.

Since we were not allowed to play with the blasting caps, our backup find was a case of metal tubes about an inch in diameter and 4 inches long, which turned out to be WWII surplus camo face paint. Mom said we could not use them, but when compared to the caps, some leeway was allowed. Two green faced boys showed up for dinner that night.

The previous owners (hoarders) had never thrown anything away, and this kept us busy for most of the first summer. To the northeast of the outbuildings ran a steep gulley. It had been the receptacle of unwanted items long before the term "landfill" was invented. At the top was the front half of a Model T Ford which was probably too heavy to get down the hill. In our make-believe adventures we kids put at least 20,000 miles on that vehicle. Also at the top were five decades of worn out tires. We couldn't believe our good fortune; no one had been smart enough to roll the tires down the gully! There was a flat rock at the base of the fence in the bottom. If a rolled tire hit the rock just right it would jump and sometimes clear the fence. Game on. We had so much fun rolling the tires down the hill that when we were done, we decided to carry them back up and roll them down again. After Larry and I each muscled a tire up the hill, we decided that it wasn't much fun anymore.

To a boy that is denied explosives, the next best thing is water, of which we had two sources, the irrigation ditch and Current Creek. The creek ran through the north end of the property and provided an endless source of entertainment. Fishing is what we did when we could not hunt. I only remember catching a few trout and ascribed this to a lack of fish, but one day a real fisherman visited our ranch and filled his creel.

While fishing near the neighbor's diversion dam we pulled out the strangest fish! It was quite large, light in color, and had a deformed mouth that looked like a suction cup on the bottom of its jaw. Even stranger was that a few minutes later we caught another one that looked the same. Before we headed home we had a dozen of them. Dad, who was no fisherman, explained that we had caught some suckers. Although I still do not consider myself a fisherman, Larry eventually became quite proficient.

With no television and only one radio station (KOVO), evenings could get a little slow. After all, we could only handle so much Dean Martin and Frank Sinatra. About dusk, Larry and I would beg dad to load us in the back of the truck with the .22. He, Mom, Cindy, and the baby (Grant) rode in the front and we were off to the alfalfa patch to find cottontails.

My first rabbit ranks as high as my first deer in terms of excitement. I now knew for a certain that the family would never go hungry. I also learned that there is a reason why rabbit season is in the winter, not the summer. While holding one of our trophy rabbits, I noticed all kinds of little bugs crawling off the rabbit and on to my arm. I don't know if they were lice or fleas or ticks, but I do know they had no business being on my arm. I recovered from the bug trauma by the next evening and was ready to go again.

A good day was when we could find a few 410 shells and half a box of .22's. Excitedly we were off to the creek to see what might develop. There were wild domestic geese, squirrels, pot guts, rabbits, and birds to pursue. We came home when it was too dark to see or we were out of shells. The day did dawn where we had no shells, not even after looking under the seat of Dad's truck. Did we sit in the cabin and complain? No, Mom would find us something to do related to cleaning the house, so we just headed for the creek.

Being unarmed bothered us for while, but while passing the garbage gulley we spied an old icebox. It was a very old type that had the compressor on the top, but the compressor was gone and all that remained was the box part. Did I say box part? I meant boat. Larry and I spent most of the morning dragging the box/boat a quarter of a mile to the launching point on the creek. We figured we would have to portage the neighbor's irrigation dam, but after that it should be a crooked shot to Red Creek, then the Strawberry River.

In our minds we could imagine eventually ending up in the Sea of Cortez. We didn't make it to Red Creek; in fact we didn't even make it to the first bend in our creek. We abandoned ship after being hung up on the second gravel bar, but vowed to attempt it again in the spring when water levels were higher.

A raft is really what we needed. We were able to find a couple of big logs and about a dozen old fence slabs. These slabs were the first piece that was cut off a log at the sawmill. One side was flat and the other side was the rounded log, some with the bark still on. The mill gave these away for free so they were a staple for corral fencing. After rummaging through the old sheds we were able to find a few handfuls of very large nails, or they might have been railroad spikes.

A few days later we had a beautiful raft, one that would have made Huckleberry Finn proud. It was amazing how heavy all of those light boards had become. Larry and I together could barely drag it a few inches at a time. Lifting one end, we were able to get a five gallon bucket under it and then we could roll it about three feet before needing to reposition the bucket. At this rate we figured we could get it to the river in about three weeks.

We didn't realize that Mom and Dad had been watching us. Lo and behold, here comes Dad on the Ford tractor. He hooked up the tow chain to the raft and while we sat on it, he pulled us to an irrigation run-off pond by Murphy's fence line. This is where the irrigation water was dumped when we didn't need it or the neighbor wasn't stealing it.

Mom waited in the truck while we spent the rest of the afternoon playing on the raft. Things went well until our dog Rover swam out to join us. The raft would only support two creatures, whether they were boys or dogs, so somebody got to go swimming. About ten years later while hiking back from deer hunting we found our old raft. Larry and Cousin Brian dragged it to the river and floated back to deer camp.

The irrigation ditch did not offer as many surprises as the creek but it was better than Mom's previous idea of cleaning the house. Our ditch originated about a mile to the east, coming out of Current Creek. The previous owner told us that the rancher upstream would probably try to steal the water since we were new, but all that was necessary was to take a shot at him with the 30-30 that everyone kept behind the seat of their truck. We assumed that he meant to shoot over his head to scare him, but after getting to know him a little better, he might not have been so generous.

Dad was at constant war with the beavers. There might be busy beavers but ours were of the lazy variety. They were lazy because they were always trying to dam our small ditch instead of tackling the bigger creek. We would go to change the irrigation water in the morning only to find a very small stream. That meant one of two things: beavers or neighbors. I have mentioned how the neighbors were handled, but it was much harder to see the beavers in order to get a shot. Initially, dad would find the dam and pull it apart. That was a lot of work, and quite often by the next morning they had the dam back in place.

One morning dad said that he heard a solution to the dam problem from another rancher. He said we were going to blow it up with dynamite. Now we are talking...explosives. I asked him if could light the fuse, just as I had seen in John Wayne movies. I was somewhat disappointed when he placed the stick of dynamite in the dam, stepped back, and pulled out the 30-30. He took careful aim, shot the dynamite, and poof - no more beaver dam. It was easier and manlier than pulling it apart with bare hands. A bonus was that either the concussion or the smell kept the beavers away for a while.

In traversing our ranch the irrigation ditch had to cross two ravines. The first was crossed with a pipe about two feet in diameter suspended about six feet above the gulley below. The second was a smaller pipe of about one foot, but it was a good twenty feet high. After we got bored of floating things down the ditch we soon dared each other to walk across the pipes. The lower pipe was soon mastered but it was near the end of the summer before we worked up the courage to cross the high culvert. I got cocky crossing the lower pipe and fairly danced across it. At the end of the pipe was a rusty old fence that had seen better days. It sagged in places and was only two feet off the ground.

If Mom wanted Dad and he was in the East field, I would run across the pipe, jump the fence and get him. One day after delivering Mom's message, I decided to jump the fence at a different place. There were two complications. The first was that the fence must have been a few inches higher than I was used to, but the second and more important, was a very large patch of prickly pear on the other side of the fence. I still remember it as if in slow motion. I jumped, caught the toe of my shoe, spread-eagled, and watched the cactus jump up to greet me.   I had spines in all of the forward facing parts of my body. It was a long run home.

The alfalfa fields below the ditch offered some amusement. We would follow behind the mower when Dad cut the hay and try to catch young cottontail rabbits, as their hiding places were laid bare. We were quite successful and sometimes got one that was slow in ducking as he had the tops of his ears clipped. We built a rabbit pen in the screened porch area of the ranch house right next to our beds. After catching a baby cottontail we would smother it with affection and make sure it was kept safe and secure. We soon noticed that if we played with them a lot they would get more and more docile but they never seemed to eat. Just when they were totally tame they disappeared. Dad said they probably got out of a hole in the cage during the night. Those cottontails must have been a lot stronger than they looked to chew through the cage wire.

There were a few Jack Rabbits and one Snowshoe Hare that lived west of the house. That Hare eluded us for years. He would sit under a lone cedar tree below the ditch west of the house, expertly judge the effective range of whatever weapon we were armed with, and vanish before he was in danger.

Occasionally, a man would stop by the ranch house and visit for a minute. We soon learned that his guy had the best job in the world. He was the government trapper. His job was to drive through the mountains and set traps for coyotes and bobcats. One day when the trapper stopped by he talked to Dad for a few minutes and then came over and asked Larry and I if we would like to help run his trap line. I had to pinch myself to make sure I hadn't died and gone to heaven.

When we reached the ridge on top of the mountain, we stopped to check the first trap. Climbing out of the truck we could see a big pile of dirt and a chain going down into a hole. The trapper had a hammer that looked kind of like a tinner's hammer with a pointed end. With a hammer in one hand, he pulled on the chain with the other. Out came a very upset badger. Although Larry and I were standing well behind the trapper, I was so surprised I nearly had to change my pants. He was able to dispatch this beast in short order.

He showed us how to reset traps by digging a small hole in the ground for the trap sit in, covering the trigger with a small piece of fabric and gently covering it with dirt. Location is everything. He put the trap between two sagebrush and in front of a third, forcing the animal to step on the trap to get to the bait in this deadly triangle. Next we went to the back of the truck to get some "scent." The "scent" was in a big metal barrel and reminded me of sour dough starter. It never runs out—you just add more of "whatever" to it. When he opened the lid I realized that the old outhouse didn't really smell that bad. I couldn't imagine what would create this kind of smell, but the trapper did say that he occasionally ground up a dead animal and added it to the brew. He took a small tin can, filled it with the scent and placed it behind the trap. He said that they could smell it a long ways away. "Like probably 10 miles," I thought.

A little while later we caught a bobcat. The cat was not happy. The trapper didn't want to waste a bullet so he unsuccessfully tried to kill the cat with his hammer. He finally gave up and tried throwing it at the cat. Now the cat was really ticked off and the hammer was inside the chain area. He asked me to go get the hammer. Being a child that always obeyed my elders I moved to pick it up. "No he shouted," as he grabbed me. "I was just joking." I wasn't too upset until I looked over at Larry, whose expression said "My big brother is an idiot."

That day I learned that the rifle is a lot more effective weapon than a hammer. I now own 15 guns and 2 hammers. That is a good ratio. After several more successful sets, we came out at Stinking Springs and soon were back home. We now had some wonderful stories and a new hobby. Larry and I couldn't wait to get to Radmall's Hardware to pick up some traps.

After purchasing the traps, we tried to mimic the lessons learned from the trapper. We set them around the ranch house and fields and were successful in catching one badger. Years later, while deer hunting, we remembered a trap we had once set (and forgot) under the shed that held the Ford tractor. We dug around and found the chain, pulled it from underneath the shed, and found the skeleton of a long-dead badger still attached.

We traveled occasionally between the ranch and our home in Pleasant Grove. If we took the truck, Dad, Mom, and the little ones rode in the front while the older kids were in the bed. In the early 60's this practice was considered safe, but in reality we didn't even think about "safe" as the truck had no seatbelts. I feel sorry for generations that will never know the feeling of traveling down highway 40, lying in the bed of a truck, covered by a sleeping bag and snuggling next to a red dog.

One time while traveling from Pleasant Grove to the ranch there was road construction in Daniels Canyon. The "stop and go" eventually took its toll on the car until we only had "stop". Mom was no mechanic but she did get the hood of the Plymouth open. As she forlornly looked at the motor, a truck of do-gooders, as dad liked to call them, pulled alongside. After taking a vote, the diagnosis was vapor-lock. One of the gentlemen took his cold beer and slowly poured it over the fuel pump. The problem was solved and we were on our way. Until I was 16 I thought you needed a beer if your car vapor-locked.

In hindsight Mom was the person that held us altogether. She was not quite five feet tall, had bright red hair and a get-it-done attitude. With humor and caring she made sure we kids felt like we were loved. We knew that Dad loved us, although his upbringing would never allow him to say the actual words. She left one of the nicest homes in Manila to assist Dad in living his dream. She traded in a real washing machine for a wringer model, a color coordinated bathroom for an outhouse, a modern kitchen for a wood stove, and a television for an AM radio. She took care of Dad and five kids in conditions that were a half a step above camping.

I never heard her complain but if you really pushed her she will admit to detesting the red dirt. It got in everything. We were required to undress on the porch and shake out our clothes before entering the ranch house, but even then enough red dirt got into the wash to make our white socks an interesting shade of pink.

As exciting as life on the ranch was for Larry and me, little sister Cindy does not have such fond memories. Maybe it was because she was quite small or maybe because she was a girl, but I think that all she remembers is the ever present dirt. One thing we could all agree on was the afternoon 2:30 ritual. No matter where our wanderings took us, we made sure to find Dad so he could load us up in the truck and head for the Fruitland General Store. We would all get a Milk Nickel ice cream, and life was good.

In 1963 while the family was in Pleasant Grove, Dad became a hero. While having morning coffee at the Lodge, he learned that some prisoners had escaped from a lumber camp in the Uintah Mountains, near Duchesne the day before. As he approached the ranch house two men came running out. They were carrying a loaf of Mom's bread, our radio, the .22, and Dad's new cowboy boots. He could understand the bread and rifle but taking his boots made it a little too personal. He retrieved the 30-30 from behind the seat, leaned over the hood of the truck, and ordered them on the ground. The man with the bread and boots complied but the man with Mom's .22 hesitated. As he turned and started to raise the .22, Dad fired a round a few inches over his head. Dad's experience with the neighbor stealing the irrigation water was becoming useful in unanticipated ways. The convict realized that he was out-gunned and hit the dirt. Dad held them at bay as the neighbors drove up to assist.

With their hands secured with bailing twine, the prisoners were taken to the nearest phone, which was located at the Lodge. The county Sheriff showed up about this time to take control of the men. As they were being loaded into the Sheriff's car, Dad told them to wait. On the ride from the ranch the convicts mentioned they hadn't eaten since yesterday. Dad told them he was going to buy them breakfast at the Lodge. Every boy needs a Dad like I had.

CHAPTER 4

FIRST DEER

I considered myself to be a knowledgeable, dedicated deer hunter, but actually shooting my first deer was a long time coming. I had participated in the hunt since I was eight and knew that when the time came I would locate a big buck, coolly judge the distance, and then make a clean, accurate shot. Reality snuck up on me, measured the distance and dealt me a clean, accurate blow. I missed the first deer that I shot at. I blamed it on Mom's Marlin 30-30 that I had borrowed, telling myself that I needed a real rifle without the rainbow trajectory.

When I turned sixteen I got a Savage model 99F in 308. The first year I didn't have a scope and I am not even sure I sighted the in the gun before the hunt. After missing a deer I learned a lifelong lesson about always knowing where my gun was shooting. There is not a better feeling than knowing when you pull the trigger the bullet will hit where you aim. Conversely, there is no worse feeling than having no idea where you are going to hit.

Dad's method of sighting in was quite straightforward. He would pace 100 steps and place a Zerex (antifreeze) can on the hill. He would then walk back to the truck, lean over the hood and shoot. If he hit it (which he always did) the Savage was considered "sighted in" and ready to go hunting.

After several unsuccessful years of deer hunting the day arrived when I knew that my luck was going to change. I had a new Bushnell 3X8 scope on my rifle, had sighted it in, and even practiced a little. It was still dark at our camp on Current Creek on opening morning as final preparations were made. Each hunter was issued a plastic Wonder Bread sack and given instructions to bring back the liver. Only about 18.2% of hunters actually like to eat liver. It is amazing how many deer ended up being shot in the liver. The excitement was palpable as a hasty breakfast of left over cookies was wolfed down and an apple was stowed away in the red sweatshirt.

We ascended the mountain in one or two pickups. The elders rode in the cab while everyone else piled in the bed. If we thought about it, a camp mattress was thrown in to cushion the bumps and jolts of the journey.

We tried to arrive at the oak brush side hill right at first light. When someone in the back saw a deer they were to lightly tap the roof of the cab to alert the driver that we wished to pause and further investigate an alleged deer sighting. What really happened was that several youngsters in the bed hammered the cab so bad that permanent dents were imprinted and semi permanent hearing loss was inflicted upon the interior occupants. After the truck slammed to a stop and everyone was thrown to the floor, the judgment of the deer commenced. A loose consensus was formed regarding the gender of the alleged deer. If the majority agreed there was indeed a buck on the hill things really ramped up.

"It's the last one on the left," "It's the second one from the right," called out the men. Once the deer was determined to be a male and its approximate location was established, the artillery was called in. At this point there were no gentlemen on the mountain; it was every nimrod for himself. It is rumored that Cousin Jay once got off three shots from the time he jumped out of the bed of the truck until his feet hit the ground, but I was there and I can only confirm two. I don't remember if we shot, or shot at, a deer that particular morning, but over the years many a deer fulfilled its destiny of initiating the jerky making process on that side hill.

Once past the oak brush side hill, the truck proceeded to drop off the occupants at a location of their choosing. They were to hunt the morning and be ready to get picked up by the truck at 11AM. The driver of the truck would start at the Grassy Knoll and proceed on the low road until he hit the corral, whereupon he would turn east and head across the high road until he turned downhill and back to camp for lunch and the first update of hunting stories (lies). The important thing about catching the truck was that if you missed it, there was a couple mile hike back to camp in the middle of the day when you were hungry and hot.

Now that the stage is set, I will return to the deer story. I remember it as being a rather slow morning and not hearing much shooting on the mountain. I was young, excited and covered a lot of country looking for that elusive first deer. I snuck up on several promising gullies that usually held deer, only to find them empty.

The holy grail of deer habitat was what we called the "Big Draw." It was the head of a large canyon that extended to the north for nearly a mile. Any deer in the area seemed to gravitate to this sacred spot. The first hunter to reach the rock ledge on the east side of the draw expected to jump several deer that were usually within range. I couldn't believe it! I was the first one to the draw. After pondering whether I would shoot a two point or wait for a bigger deer I was brought back to reality by the sound of the deer gods laughing at me. They thought it quite funny to scare off the large buck that surely was there shortly before I arrived.

After the Big Draw disappointment I looked at my watch and found that it was almost 11AM, so I headed back to the Grassy Knoll via the country between the high and low roads. From the time I first was "allowed" to participate in the holy event of the deer hunt, our camp had certain rules and protocol to follow. As mentioned, rule #1 was no women, rule #2 was the minimum age of eight, and #3 was that the truck going back to camp leaves the Grassy Knoll at 11AM sharp.

A deer hunter's awareness seems to ebb the further the sun rises. Excitement is high when it is just getting light enough to see and the next hour is golden in many ways, but by

11AM the dreams for the morning are almost dead. I was hot, tired, and a little dejected when, to my complete and utter surprise, two bucks jumped from the brush about 100 yards in front of me. I could tell immediately that they were "shooters," meaning that I could see horns through my scope. I quickly brought up the Savage and took it off safe.

Dad did not believe in binoculars so we learned to hunt deer a lot like we hunted pheasants. We would cover a lot of ground and flush them like so many birds. If you weren't quick on the draw you either missed the close shot or even worse, the guy next to you got it.

I was young and not as experienced so I usually had a cartridge in the chamber. The gun came up like it was a part of me, as soon as the bigger buck got into the crosshairs I squeezed one off. It felt good so I diverted my attention to the other buck to see which direction he was going. He was dropping into the Wild Strawberry side so I knew none of our group would want to chase him in that wilderness.

I now turned my attention to retrieving my "first" deer. I walked over to where I thought I last saw him and started looking. He was not where I remembered him to be. About this time I remember hearing the truck making the homeward loop. I didn't want to miss the truck,

I wasn't too worried about walking back to camp but I really needed for everyone to see my trophy. The dilemma was that the way it was shaping up, I was going to miss the truck and not find my deer. After what seemed like an hour, but was probably closer to 10 minutes I rounded some oak brush and almost tripped over the deer.

Non hunters will never know the relief of finding an animal that was thought to have been lost.

My attention now turned to remembering exactly what Dad had done while gutting a deer. It took quite a while but eventually I got the job done. Unfortunately I had shot him in the liver. The larger of the two "shooter" bucks was the one that I dropped. He turned out to be a real nice spike and I was never more proud of any deer I have taken. The 2 mile walk to camp with red hands was a pleasure walk.

CHAPTER 5

Larry's Spike

There are few things more humiliating when you are young than to have your younger brother show you up. I was eighteen and my brother Larry was sixteen when we decided to drive to Fruitland for the second weekend of the rifle deer hunt. Fruitland was considered winter range for the deer herd so the later in the season you hunted the better your odds were. We were just going to do a day hunt, so very early on the second Saturday, Brother Larry, Cousin Dave, my girlfriend (Lynne) and I loaded up dad's Ford two wheel drive pickup and set off with high hopes.

NOTE: After consulting with Larry to verify the accuracy of the story, he pointed out that it was not the second Saturday, but was in fact the second Sunday, which puts me in the uncomfortable situation of having to confess the sin of hunting on the Sabbath. As I have grown older my comfort level of Sabbath day observance has had a few ups and downs, with the general direction pointing to more of what the Lord has directed. About the time that my personal commitment to not hunting on Sunday started increasing I observed a remarkable change in the outcome of my hunts. The change was that I didn't seem to get as many deer.

Arriving in Fruitland at daylight we found a few inches of snow near Current Creek, so through past experience we knew that there would be anywhere from six inches to a foot of the white stuff on top.

There are not many things more manly than chaining up a truck, so we proceeded to make the truck invincible in the snow. The approved chain up spot for generations to come was the "Lambing Shed." When we moved into the log ranch house in 1961 every building on the property except the lambing shed was at least 50 years old. Being made of remnant sawmill slabs, the shed was still new and shiny. It was only weather proof enough to keep the rain off of the new born lambs. If we could make it to the shed it was the ideal place to put the chains on in a dry, if somewhat dusty place.

We plowed through the snow along the irrigation ditch, turned uphill to the spring road and went left, rounded Cedar Point, turned at the Porcupine Tree (or stump, depending on how old you are), turned right at the Maple Springs cutoff, across the hogs back, veered right to the low road, another right toward the pines and stopped at the Grassy Knoll. None of the names I just mentioned can be found on a USGS map, but since we thought we pioneered this mountain it was only fitting that we should name the prominent features.

We parked at the Grassy Knoll and designed a plan of attack upon the unsuspecting deer of Lower Current Creek Mountain. Actually, we were now drawing up our backup plan because our first preference was to find a couple of deer close enough to the road to make an easy drag but not so close as to be accused of being "road hunters."

The backup plan was for Larry and Cousin Dave to take the low route and for Lynne and me to take the high route. We would push the gullies until we met at the head of the Big Draw and then decide how to circle back to the truck.

Lynne and I waited for a while, but Larry and Dave never showed up at the Big Draw, so we hiked to the corral. As mentioned in a previous chapter the agreed upon time to be back at the truck was 11AM. There were no other hunters with us so it really didn't matter when we met, but tradition dies hard. From the corral we made a large circle above the high road and were back to the truck with a few minutes to spare.

At the truck we shook the snow off, had a snack, and waited for the guys to get back. A half an hour went by and they were not back, then another, and another. About 1:00 we figured something was wrong and we better start looking for them.

You might wonder why I waited for two hours before taking off. I was alone with a beautiful woman and decided I would only give them about four more hours, but since we were running low on gas and the darn windows kept fogging up I decided to move on.

The snow was fairly deep where we were parked so we carefully went west to the junction of the high road and turned left at the pole corral. After traveling East on the high road we retraced our morning route down the mountain. We searched all the possible spots on the mountain to no avail.

A couple of hours later while going west on the spring road, we found the boys in the cedars walking toward us. Dave said he had just shot a "nice" doe so we drove a short distance and loaded it up. It was getting later in the afternoon and I was ready to head home when Larry informed us that he had shot a spike up on top, west of the Big Draw. I wasn't crazy about going up the mountain again on the slick trail but I remembered with nostalgia the feeling I experienced after shooting my first buck. Lynne, Larry and I got in the cab while Dave offered to ride in the bed with his deer.

The chains bit into the snow and with rear wheels spinning we once again went up the mountain, past the Big Draw, and onto ground that I had never hunted. I stopped at the top of a steep hill, not being too sure if I could get back up even with the chains on. Larry said the deer was only a couple of hundred yards away, so we parked and prepared to go get his spike. He said he was going to get a rope to help drag the deer and I replied that since it was only a spike I would just throw it on my back and carry it to the truck. I am sure I would have said the same thing even if my girlfriend was not looking admiringly at me. Larry grabbed the rope anyway.

He led us down the hill into the head of a canyon filled with quakies. This spot was to be named years later as Reese's Rock in honor of a hunting buddy who seemed to always get a buck or two there. In hindsight I can almost hear

Larry and Dave stifling chuckles as we approached the "spike." As we rounded some brush at the top of the gulley his deer came into view. It was the largest deer both in antlers and weight that I had ever seen. The antlers were a tall, heavy 4 point and the deer weighed at least 230 pounds gutted.

Two of us grabbed a horn and the other harnessed himself into the rope. The drag to the truck began. The difficulty of the uphill deer recovery effort was compounded by the fact that two of the men were on the short side of five feet tall and couldn't rotate the scales to the 100 pound mark.

After hours of dragging, (or maybe one half hour), we arrived at the Ford and struggled to get the beast into the bed of the truck. If there had not been a young lady present I don't know if we could have done it. With darkness closing in, we headed down the mountain and listened to Larry and Dave's story.

In the morning they must have arrived at the Big Draw first and when they did not see us, they just kept going. A little to the west a doe popped up at about 75 yards. Larry was armed with mom's Marlin 30-30 while Dave had Grandma Colledge's Winchester 30-30. Dave wanted to take home some venison, so he carefully aimed and shot, and shot, and shot.

Grandma's gun held about 7 rounds and Cousin Dave was grateful for the large magazine capacity.

As the deer ran away he said that he had hit it. Larry was somewhat skeptical, but like true sportsmen they advanced to look for blood. Surprise! A few drops of blood were evident in the snow. One of his shots barely missed the heart and hit the deer in the hoof. With a faint blood trail and good tracks they followed in warm pursuit. They would have followed in "hot" pursuit but couldn't because it was just too darn cold.

Another mile to the west the tracks lead them through the head of the previously mentioned quakies. They were following the tracks up the far side when Larry's big buck snuck out from behind them. It had been hiding and thought it was safe from two small 16 year olds with open sighted 30-30s. Larry threw mom's rifle up, drew a "fine" bead, and squeezed off a well-placed shot. Well, the shot would have been well-placed if he had been shooting at the neck, and to this day he still claims that was where he was aiming. Because of Larry a new policy was instituted in our camp requiring hunters to "call" head and neck shots in advance.

After gutting the monarch they picked up the doe's trail and pressed on. The pursuit took them down the Radio Tower canyon into the cedars and back east. They tracked the deer for about four miles and were getting just a little discouraged when they spotted the doe. Dave took careful aim and shot, and shot, etc. After he emptied his 30-30 Larry handed him his gun and reminded him to take a "fine" bead.

Growing up the only instructions Dad would give up when shooting open sights was to draw a fine bead. I was older when I figured the logic behind his counsel. When you are excited the natural tendency is to shoot before the front sight (bead) is resting in the bottom of the back sight which increases the odds of missing.

After a couple of more shots Dave claimed his prize. Dave looked at Larry and said, "I know you don't approve but I have just got to have a smoke," which explains why he wanted to ride in the back of the truck when we found them a short time later.

It was exciting going home to show off the results of a successful hunt. A crowd gathered, congratulations were enviously handed out and memories were made. Larry's deer is still one of the largest I have ever seen in hunting for over 50 years. His deer was quite a contrast to my first deer. Mine really was a spike.

Although in the beginning of this narrative I said it was humiliating having my younger brother show me up, after reliving this experience I have nothing but good memories.

THE DEER HUNTER'S OATH

CHAPTER 6

MUZZLE LOADING

We originally started muzzle hunting so we could squeak out another couple of weeks of deer hunting each year, not because we were mountain men. The deer muzzleloader used to follow the rifle season, which was perfect for the lower winter range that we liked to hunt.

There were days that we would see two or three hundred head of deer but the buck/doe ratio being was somewhere between one and two bucks per 100 does. We looked at a lot of deer to find anything with horns. My theory for the extremely low ratios was that the area we hunted was so accessible that any deer with antlers above its ears was road-hunted and shot during the rifle season. A secondary contributing factor was that if you considered yourself a "local," the normal game laws regarding seasons and bag limits did not apply to you.

Our previous experience with muzzle loading was limited to a pair of pistols. The first was an early 1800's replica that came in a kit. After assembling and firing it we determined that it was a miracle that the early colonists pushed the Indians out of their native lands. Its effective range to hit a man-sized target was less than twenty feet.

The second was a six shot revolver. It took about ten minutes to correctly load the cylinders, so we did it in five. The reason we loaded it so quickly was that we didn't seal the cylinder ends with grease as instructed. The result was that upon firing at least one and maybe more adjacent cylinders would sympathetically go off. If you were lucky only the gun was blown to the ground and not a few of your fingers.

For the first few years we borrowed rifles for the muzzle load season. One was a Hawken style 50 caliber, one a Green River Long Rifle of 45 caliber, and the last was 58 caliber Zouave. The owners were somewhat negligent in educating us as to their operation. We guessed how much powder to put in, found a ball of approximate diameter, primed it, pointed it in the general direction of the deer, pulled the trigger and were disappointed.

As dismal as our hunting results were, the opportunity of having one more excuse to be on the mountain before winter set in motivated us to get our own guns. We started with Hawken kits of various calibers. Larry had a 54, Gordon had a 45, and I chose a 50. A discussion ensued regarding the relative significance of manliness versus caliber but was tabled when Bob Hansen showed up with his Zouave.

Throughout the winter the guns were crafted, and by summer we were experimenting with different powder/ball/slug combinations. With our very own, hand-built rifles we were ready to start hunting.

When I was in college I ended up HAVING to get married.... I was starving to death. If not for Pete's Spudnut Shop in Logan I would not have survived. Many of my brothers followed suit. Larry must have not been as good looking as the rest of us since he married later in life. In addition to not spending money on dates it afforded him the opportunity to perfect his cooking skills. Because of him the muzzle load season developed into quite a culinary extravaganza.

Every year Larry would try to outdo himself. One year it was a honey baked ham, another was a prime rib, slow cooked to perfection, and another time it was a full blown turkey-type Thanksgiving dinner. We were very grateful to Larry for the food, but it also kept him occupied and gave the rest of us more time to hunt.

After Larry's dinner it was time to prepare for the morning hunt. Guns were cleaned, powder was measured and slugs were stored in a convenient place. I have always liked the smell of gunpowder but found out quickly that I like the smell of "Smokeless Powder." Black powder has sulfur in it and is not pleasant. While measuring the charges, some powder always seemed to spill or there was a need to dispose of last year's stale powder.

One time while staying in the cabin an unknown hunter collected the left over powder, wrapped it in a piece of metal foil left over from the baked potatoes and, while no one was looking, threw it in the wood stove. Nothing happened for a few minutes and just as the culprit thought his prank was not going to work an explosion blew the door off of the stove. The cabin filled with smoke and embers as the occupants tried to recover their dignity by saying that it didn't scare them at all.

While loading your gun you never left it unattended during the process. If you did, someone would slip in an extra measure of powder and you would only discover the tampering after picking yourself up from the ground after ignition.

Our early muzzle loading experiences taught us the value of "keeping your powder dry." We had often heard this trite term but gained new appreciation of it when we got a big buck in our sights and had only the cap go off with no following BOOM. The only thing worse than a misfire is a "hang fire." A hang fire is when the cap goes off and there is a delayed reaction until the main powder charge ignites. This phenomenon can take from milliseconds to 10 seconds.

We learned very early that if the charge did not ignite immediately, point the gun at an inanimate object, close your eyes, and pray. If your gun hangfires and you lower it before it goes off you will hit the ground somewhere beneath the deer. With some of our poor shooters the hangfire might actually improve their odds of hitting the deer.

Before we had actually shot a deer with these primitive weapons we thought that the large chunk of lead would knock a deer right off of his hooves. With a slug that big even a poor shot should put a deer down. We were having a great time driving to the top of the mountain, educating a brand new hunter and retelling our old stories. Lynn Beckstead was a co-worker of Larry's and one of his old missionary friends. Lynn was very curious as to how accurate the guns were and, of course, we downplayed our skills.

We were about half way up the mountain when we spotted a group of deer a little over 100 yards away, running down the gully opposite us. They were on my side so I stepped out to look them over. Grant hollered that the last one was a buck so I threw up the 50 Caliber Hawken, aimed at the biggest part and fired. At the shot, the deer dropped like no other I had ever seen. "Boy, these muzzle loaders really pack a wallop." Was Lynn ever impressed. He thought I was the best shot in the world. He had never even gotten his gun out of the truck.

We hiked over to the deer and I started getting nervous. The deer's head was partially in a sage brush and I couldn't see any antlers. I was sure that I had seen them but now I was second guessing myself.

As we pulled the buck from the brush there was an antler hidden underneath the sage. The side of the deer's head that was first visible had a hole in its ear and the antler had been shot off earlier in the rifle hunt. Now that I was not feeling as sick over having come close to committing the unpardonable...shooting a doe... we started to look at the damage that the half inch slug had done. It is true that this would have been a "good shot" if I had been aiming at the deer's head, because that is where the hole was, but since I hadn't "called" the head shot my companions classified this as a "bad shot".

After the first season the factory sights were replaced with peep sights and our comfort level increased. As we slowly perfected the art, the time eventually came when we were somewhat confident of hitting what we were aiming at within reasonable ranges.

It is one thing to miss a deer for whatever reason but quite another to never even get the slug down range. I have witnessed and may have participated in the fiasco unique to muzzle loading where you dump in the powder, put on a cap, and fire, having forgotten the somewhat important step of putting the slug down the barrel. When a shot like this is taken it is extremely hard to kill the deer. This usually happens on a shot subsequent to the first, in the heat of battle. Although I might have done this once, I think Gordon perfected it.

We were pushing the basin west of the Big Draw when a buck jumped from cover and bolted away from the closest hunter, which happened to be Gordy. He casually raised his Hawken and made what first appeared to be a good shot. By good, I mean that the deer only ran a short distance in Larry's direction before dropping. As Larry walked toward the deer it miraculously resurrected and, with difficulty, started rising to its feet. Gordon shouted to Larry to shoot it again, but Larry later stated that he didn't want to ruin the liver and was sure that it was not going far. As the deer gained strength it started a hobbling walk and then with a burst of new-found life took off on a dead run. It was never to be seen again.

A trial was later convened around the campfire and Larry was found guilty of not following the deer hunting policy of, "keep killing them until they are dead". Gordon was severely reprimanded for using a "woman's gun" of only 45 caliber. If either infraction had been avoided, the children would not have had to go hungry that winter.

Grant Ferre joined us on our annual hunt one year. He had never shot a muzzle loader before and instead of getting the good Hawken he got a cheap imitation. The night before the hunt we taught him how to load the gun and then sighted it in for him. Just as we finished sighting it in, the front site fell off. We put it back on with a piece of duct tape. It was now too dark to test the accuracy, but who cared, it was just for Ferre.

The next morning we were off to the hunt. Shortly after splitting up we heard a shot from Ferre's direction. Concerned that he might have shot himself in the foot we investigated, and quite to our surprise, found him standing over the buck he had just killed. We took solace in the fact that we must have been very good teachers.

Over the years some of us who are more into hunting than being a mountain man have upgraded our arsenal. We have traded in the Hawken for one of the more accurate inline rifles. With the new powder pellets, saboted slugs, and shotgun primers, the sights are the only limitation.

No matter what style of rifle you use, at the end of the night you need to unload it. It is possible to pull the slug and empty the powder, but the safer and manlier way is to just shoot it. When it becomes too dark to hunt we usually point the gun at a dirt bank and discharge it into the ground. This was fun, but our curious minds eventually degenerated to wondering if we shot it straight up could we hear the slug fall to the earth. After many such trials we did hear the slug hit. It hit about three feet from the windshield of the truck. We don't do that anymore.

CHAPTER 7

IT WASN'T TECHNICALLY ROAD HUNTING

In most hunting circles, a "road hunter" is held in contempt and derision. Our camp subscribed loosely to this philosophy. I say "loosely" because we had a very large area to hunt and not much time to hunt it. We had hunted Fruitland for generations and knew the areas that the deer liked. The problem was that the prime areas were usually some distance from each other. The system that developed was one where we would drive to a good spot and make a circle hike or get dropped off, hike to a predetermined location, and then get picked up. This system served us well but we had a difficult time closing our eyes and not looking out the window while traveling to the next hunting spot.

One fine November day Gordy, Grant, and I were in "Big Red" traveling to the rim rock overlook west of the Big Draw. Note: In the eighties it was fashionable to name an especially loved or tolerated vehicle. A few that come to mind are "Old Yeller", "The Bird," and perhaps my favorite, "Mahana". Big Red was a 1979 Ford highboy F250 Supercab, long bed 4X4 and, of course, was red. The paint was red, the rust was red, and the transmission oil that dripped was red. It took us to, and usually home, from some great adventures.

We were on an old two track trail just making the north turn to the rim rock when I spotted something in the oak brush ahead and to the left. It was white and looked out of place. Of course when you are deer hunting anything white is a potential deer's rear end. It intrigued me enough to stop and bring up the binoculars.

My dad never had much use for binoculars. He said, if you can't see horns it is not big enough to shoot, which is an interesting statement from a man who shot his share of spikes and two points. I, however, had read a lot of Jack O'Conner and was a firm believer in the power of optics. This sometimes worked against me since I was the spotter and didn't get in on the first shot. As the binos found the white spot it was not a rear end, but a deer's white face. I started to dismiss the animal as being just another doe when someone said "I think it is a buck."

By now I had the spotting scope up and coming into focus. Normally I look for small antlers right above the head but to my astonishment this deer had horns out past his ears! I yelled, "It's a BIG buck", and it was every man for himself. I settled the front sight on the mighty stag, pulled the "set" trigger on the Hawken, and then lightly touched the main trigger. A cloud of black powder smoke obscured my vision for a moment and then I yelled, "I got him."

A complication soon developed since both Gordy and Grant were saying that "they" had got him. Apparently we all three had fired at essentially the same time and did not hear the others fire. The deer was down but not out. We had hit him a little far back, which is code for either a gut or rear end shot.

A plan immediately developed to surround the deer and move in on him. As the circle tightened the deer started to recover. He stood up, then started walking, and then picked up steam and started right for me. I waited until he was about 40 yards away and shot directly into his brisket. The moment I squeezed the trigger the deer's front legs dropped into an unseen wash lowering his front half so the slug hit him in the left eye.

Pandemonium erupted. On the ground in front of us lay the largest deer to come off the mountain in 25 years. He was a 28 inch 4X4 with a few kickers. It was the deer that dreams are made of, and he was taken with a Hawken muzzle loader. After the initial shock wore off a few subtle comments started to surface. Grant: "You know, my sights were dead on when I shot." Gordy: "My shot just felt real good." I informed them that we were not sure who "wounded" the deer, but we do know who "killed" it.

Later on while skinning the trophy we found the initial slug that slowed the deer down enough to eventually claim him. If not for this first shot he would have escaped forever. We had an interesting dilemma. We were shooting different calibers and different bullets so it would be possible to see who really got the deer. I held the slug in my hand and looked at my brothers. We came to an agreement without saying a word and I threw it as far as I could. It was now **all** our deer.

Currently it is a traveling trophy and has been in several states. I (or rather my wife) have had it long enough. I think it is Gordy's turn.

CHAPTER 8

DOE KILLER

At the top of the dugway were two steel posts with a cable stretched across them. The cable went through the post and was hooked with a big lock. For the three years we had the ranch, we owned the key, but after that we had to get it from the people who were leasing the ground. We considered the mountain ours, and after all, it was the holy grail of deer hunting. The task of procuring the key each year went to Dad.

I remember each year as we were getting ready to leave on the hunt, Bert and Charlie would ask him if he had the key. Most of the time, a week or two before the hunt, Dad had made a visit to the neighbors and picked it up. One year Dad did not have the key when we left and told us that he had to go get it. As he got ready to drive over he reached behind the seat of his truck and got a bottle of Jack Daniels out of a brown paper bag. Dad wasn't a drinker so we were a little confused. Come to find out, the key wasn't free. Dad told us that this was a yearly ritual, a bottle for the key. People now pay thousands of dollars to access a good deer hunting area that in the 60's cost a bottle of whiskey.

With the lock opened and camp established, we were now prepared for the opening morning. As we pulled up to the Grassy Knoll to park we observed a half dozen does between us and the low road. By now I was into powerful though inexpensive binoculars. I bought the Bushnell 10X50's because I could afford them and they had a lifetime warranty which I took full advantage of several times. We desperately tried to find antlers but even with the aid of the binoculars we were unsuccessful.

Forgetting about the does, we were just starting on our various hikes when we heared the unmistakable sound of a VW beetle moving slowly down the low road. We were not surprised when he slammed on his brakes to check out the does we had just been watching. I had taken about twenty steps when I heard a rifle shot come from the low road near the beetle. Was there a small buck in the group that we had missed?

I saw a man leave the VW and run over to his buck. He took one look and instead of gutting it he quickly turned around a made a beeline to his bug, fired up all four air cooled cylinders and headed west in a cloud of dust on the low road. Our curiosity was now piqued so we hiked up to the deer he shot and saw it was a doe. I don't know what he was thinking because he could still see us, and if there was a buck we would have already got it.

He now had two issues: one, he had just illegally shot a doe and two, he was driving a very unmanly hunting vehicle. His actions would have been understandable the year before when it was legal to shoot either sex, but this year the law had changed to buck only, making does illegal to kill, and him a poacher.

We were upset. With much harrumphing and just the right amount of righteous indignation we all agreed that there is no lower form of man than that of a "Doe Killer," and some day he would get his!

Grant and I both hiked west and met up at the head of the Big Draw. The only thing we saw was the VW bug parked right above our destination. We once again cursed the doe killer and started down the hogs back toward the spring. There are only a few ways to get down the hogs back and we soon came across a unique set of boot tracks. They were of the Vibram type which was quite new to our area. A quick back track revealed the boot prints were in fact made by Mr. Doe Killer himself.

We followed his tracks until he turned to the northeast and entered some pines. We were standing on the rim rock just above the spring and facing west, wondering where to go next, when we heard something running beneath our perch. A monster buck broke out of the brush about 175 yards below and to the north of us. We didn't need binoculars to see that this buck was a definite shooter and he was moving like a cat with its tail on fire.

(When we were young a neighbor kid dipped the tip of a stray cat's tail in gas and then lit it to see what it would do. What it did was to run directly into their hay barn and within a very short time the barn was blazing merrily away. I am sure the cat escaped with only minor injuries but the barn vanished.)

The deer was running flat out as it entered a small clearing about 50 yards wide. We would have time for only one shot each. Grant took a quick offhand shot before the deer got through the clearing. He missed. I gambled on having enough time to sit my butt down, got as steady as I could, lead the buck by about a foot, and jerked the trigger. Everyone thinks they squeeze the trigger, but I was lucky enough to jerk at just the right moment.

To our surprise, at my shot the buck dropped and skidded to a stop. We let out a holler then Grant and I slid down the steep rock face with our feet only occasionally touching the ground. When a big buck goes down I am always worried that it will catch its breath and run away, so we raced to make sure it would not get back up. Our fears were groundless, for when we got closer we found that the shot had broken its neck.

The excitement of downing the biggest deer I had ever seen was tempered only slightly by the fact that I had misjudged the shot placement. Since the deer was running, I thought I needed to lead it (like when shooting at a duck) when in reality it needed only a small adjustment. I hit it very close to where I had aimed. As I have mentioned previously, in our camp you are required to "call" head and neck shots.

In those days we never thought of taking pictures, so the next order of business was to cut its throat. We cut their throat because that is what Dad had always done. The logic was that a deer needed to have its throat cut to bleed out.

Since then we have determined that the deer has usually bled out before we get to it. For the first time I was considering having the head mounted so we decided to forgo the throat cutting, which was to bring me some grief from the older members of our camp because of the obvious breech of deer dressing etiquette.

The adrenaline had almost dropped to a manageable level when we saw a hunter striding toward us with a purpose. He looked at us with distain and informed us that we had just shot "his" buck. He said that he had been tracking the deer in the pines for most of the morning. I think he actually wanted us to give him the deer. In reality he had spooked the deer towards us. Judging by the amount of time he took to reach us, the deer would have been halfway to Heber if we had not shot it.

The adrenaline was ramping up again when I happened to look at his boots. They had Vibram soles. I looked him in the eye and asked, "Aren't you the guy that shot the doe on top this morning?" He got a sick look on his face, spun on his heel and took off without saying another word.

The buck was a heavy 5X4 about 25 inches wide. For years I thought I would never again get a deer that big. I really thought my wife liked it, so it hung in honor in our home until years later when she let me know that it clashed with her interior decorating theme. It now looks down on me at work.

CHAPTER 9

TWO SHOOTER

We always considered that we "owned" the mountain where we hunted deer in Fruitland. We actually only owned about 1,000 acres of mainly farmland and cedars for a period of about three years in the early 60's. The sheep herder that owned the adjacent 5,000 acres had allegedly given us permission to hunt his property in 1960, so as far as we are concerned it is still in effect today.

In 1978 while hiking back to the river because I had missed the 11AM truck to camp, I was offered a ride by a hunter named Reese. He was friendly, but wanted to know if I knew that I was on "private property." I informed him that I did indeed know that it was private but that we had permission to hunt. He told me that he was in the process of purchasing the mountain but since I had a previous relationship he would allow us to keep hunting.

Reese was actually a very good salesman and before the next hunting season rolled around he had sold me a ten acre lot on the mountain where I had previously hunted for free. Reese and I hit it off and became hunting buddies. The relationship lasted for many years.

While Reese and I rode around the mountain in one of our trucks NOT "road hunting," we would occasionally see a deer that needed shooting. We usually took turns, but eventually it happened that we both thought it was our turn. The magnitude of the disagreement regarding shooting order was directly proportional to the size of the antlers.

One time when the proper order could not be established Reese suggested that we both shoot on the count of three. We both got on target and counted, One, Two, BOOM, Three. Reese inducted me into the two shooter club by not waiting for the full count of three, but shooting on the count of two. I was upset, but couldn't wait until I could initiate my brothers into the club.

After teaching my brothers about the Two Shooting concept we unanimously decided that it should be adopted into our camp's code of conduct. Whenever a new hunter, or a new-to-us hunter showed up it was our duty to educate him about the geography, customs and etiquette of our camp. This learning process came faster to some than others, and when the "new guy's" frustration was not self-inflicted it was the considered duty of the older, wiser hunters to assist the novice along his journey. One of the first lessons to be taught was to educate him about the lowest form of hunter, the "Two Shooter."

The position of Two Shooter teacher was highly sought after, and sometimes if conditions were favorable, several hunters could participate in the counting ritual at the same time. The Two Shooter lesson works well in other forms of hunting but especially when shooting ducks over decoys.

The Two Shooter experience, along with the Deer Hunter's Oath, have become necessary rites of deer camp. The derogatory term "Two Shooter" has stood the test of time and ranks only a little lower than that of "Daily Bather," and somewhat above "Doe Killer" in our camp.

CHAPTER 10

FISHLAKE

In the late seventies Reese introduced us to new deer hunting territory outside of the Uintah Basin. He talked of a place that had dozens of bucks running together. Indeed it would be hard to throw a rock and not hit a deer. We didn't believe him. I had never seen more than two bucks together at one time in my life.

I hadn't bow hunted for years, but Reese talked me into starting up again at a place called Fishlake. I had heard about fishing in Fishlake from my Grandpa and Mom but had never hunted there.

Reese, Gordon, Uncle Greg, and a few friends made the pilgrimage to the holy place. While Reese and I motored up Mount Terrell Gord and his bunch followed slowly in Mom's Ford Fiesta. We noticed that the Fiesta was not keeping up. Since we were in four wheel drive, we change plans and went back to get them. We found a lovely spot on a barren, windy slope to pitch camp. Just before dusk I hiked to the top of the hill and glassed for miles to the east. I couldn't believe it, Reese was right!! Directly below me were eight bucks placidly feeding. Down the ridge to the north I saw a dozen more bucks, with one of them pushing thirty inches. As it grew dark I kept finding more and more deer. I didn't sleep well that night dreaming of the deer I would see on the opening tomorrow morning.

The wind blew all night and kept up the next morning. I got close to several bucks but not close enough for a shot. In the afternoon the wind had died down so I tried to sneak into a canyon where I had seen deer on the morning hike. There was a 25 inch four point bedded down about 200 yards away in the tall grass. I slowly crept toward him and after an hour had closed to within about sixty yards. I was now getting close to where I would be comfortable if the right shot presented itself. As I was trying to get just a little bit closer all hell broke loose. My buck and five others that were apparently bedded with him all took off running. At least where I had previously hunted you didn't have to worry about the logistics of sneaking up on twelve eyes and ears.

A few years later found me near the above location. I had spotted a group of deer approaching me from below. I was actually too close to the trail, and if they stayed on course they would pass by me within a few yards. There were three smaller bucks, a 24 incher, and a doe, walking in that order. I nervously waited as they got closer and closer. The three small bucks passed by me and then the bigger one. If the doe got by me with no alarm I could take a ten yard shot at the big buck. The doe went by the bush that concealed me and stopped. She turned around, looked me in the eye, laughed, spoke something in deer language to the rest of the herd, and they all bolted away.

In total frustration I stood and loudly cursed the Deer Gods. As I turned to walk back to camp I noticed a deer about one hundred yards away standing on a trail that had been out of my view. While I was concentrating on the deer that had just run off he had been approaching me and would have offered an even better shot if I had been prepared for him. He looked at me, snorted, turned and WALKED away. Incidentally, he was a thirty inch 4X4.

We were over 11,000 feet up Mount Terrell on the bow hunt enjoying the high country when Gordy saw a string of five bucks on a trail below him moving toward the pass. If he hurried he could intercept them and get a shot at one of the four points in the group. He ran as fast as his little legs would carry him (he is the shortest of the brothers and we make sure that he does not forget it.) He arrived breathless just as the last buck entered the pass.

Usually the wise, old mature buck is the last one since he has learned to let the younger and dumber deer go first into unforeseen danger. Unfortunately, today the smart deer was only a two point, and maybe he really wasn't that smart after all.

Gordy pulled back his PSE compound, aligned the appropriate pin and let the arrow fly. We don't know if it was the wind, or the deer's movement, or maybe the rotation of the earth, but the arrow drifted, hitting the deer a little far back. "A little" in this context is about two and a half feet. As the arrow stuck in his rear end, the deer wheeled around and headed down the trail it had just come up.

If Gord felt bad about the poor shot he felt even worse when, after about three bounces, the arrow fell out of the deer. As he was thinking of which excuse he would use when he got back for lunch, the deer started slowing down, then walked, then stopped, then fell over. He didn't need to delve into his excuse file at all because he had wisely cut the femoral artery making this into a "good shot".

A week before the opening of the rifle deer hunt, the boys and I went to Fishlake with the Pyne boys. We had elk tags in our pockets but were really more interested in scouting up a big buck for the next Saturday. We arrived Friday afternoon and, after setting up the tents, we each took a basin to see if we could find a mature deer.

My boys and I hiked into the basin that lies below the Red Knob and were soon seeing deer. After working our way south for about an hour we turned around to head back to camp before it got dark. It was just about dusk when we saw him. He was 300 yards below the Red Knob feeding at the edge of a small patch of pines. We got a good look at him and determined that he was a heavy 4X4 that was at least 28 inches. He didn't see us, so we skirted the hill and made it back to camp without spooking him.

The next day we switched basins and Jeff Pyne scouted the area that we had covered the night before. We meet back at camp to eat lunch and trade notes. Jeff had seen the same 28 incher in about the same place as we had. Between the two basins we had seen about two dozen bucks with at least five of them being larger mature deer.

We could hardly wait for next week. The area we hunt is over 11,000 feet so it is not every year that you can get up the mountain late in October. Luckily the weather was mild so the next Friday found us in the same camp spot preparing for opening day. The Red Knob was one of the more popular spots and I thought that someone would for sure sit on it and spook whatever was there. I planned to setup downhill where the big buck would likely run to when the Red Knob sitter spooked him.

Daylight came and I scrutinized every path the deer could take when he came down the hill to us. I had a big boulder for a rest and we were ticking off the minutes until he peeked through the trees. I had most of the boys with me and here was their chance to see the old man drop the big one. We waited and waited and waited, but he never made the grand entry. A week ago we saw a dozen bucks in this basin, but on opening morning all that moved was a lone coyote. The boys were looking for excitement and urged me to dispatch the coyote. If all dogs go to heaven then this one surely made the trip that morning.

As we were eating lunch back at camp and wondering where all the deer had gone the boys commented that they had never hiked to the top of Mount Terrell. We decided that we would make the climb after resting up a bit. Our route up the mountain took us past the Red Knob. When we reached it I showed the boys the patch of trees that the big buck was in last week. It was about two in the afternoon and I couldn't believe what I saw. Our deer was calmly feeding in the edge of the trees, not twenty feet from where we had seen him the previous week, and he did not know we were there.

It was a fairly long shot of about 300 yards but with my 257 Weatherby and a prone position I was already trying to decide if I wanted the deer mounted facing left or right. I steadied the gun and squeezed the trigger. At the shot the deer jumped into the trees immediately behind him and went out of view. I told the boys, "let's walk down and get our deer."

Everyone was excited right up to the point where after an hour of looking, I was forced to admit that I had missed it. Apparently I had not allowed enough for the steep downhill angle and had shot right over his back. I can usually make up an excuse for not making a shot but this one still haunts me.

My neighbor Bill was curious about my stories of Fishlake and wanted to see for himself. After making camp one bow hunt I gave him a short tutorial on the mountain and some recommended places he might hunt. He decided to go south over the Rabbit Ears pass and try the next basin. It was a grueling hike but he was young and in better shape than now. He came back to camp later in the day disheveled, shaken, and with this sad story.

He was hiking down a well-worn trail when he spotted a buck coming towards him on the same trail. The hillside was wide open except for a small pine tree a few feet off the trail. His plan was to hide behind the tree until the deer came within range and then step out and shoot it. The problem was that when he was behind the tree he would not be able to see the deer until it was almost on top of him. The timing needed to be perfect.

The deer was in no hurry so Bill hid and patiently waited. Presently, he heard footsteps coming down the trail. He carefully calculated all the variables, drew his bow and stepped from behind the tree into the trail. He calculated most of the variables correctly except the one that included the deer's forward progress. The deer was not the anticipated 20 yards away, but only two feet. The startled deer, which had picked up speed, didn't have time to slow down, veer, or turn around, so it ran right over the top of poor Bill. We still sit around the campfire and argue who was more scared. In his honor we now refer to this place as Bill's Basin.

CHAPTER 11

REDTOP

My brother Grant moved away from Utah several decades ago. Some say he wanted to see the world, others say he found a better job, and even others say that his departure was precipitated by the now infamous doe incident, but personally I think he went just far enough away to where he could be a Bishop.

He eventually settled in Laramie, Wyoming where the process of picking a new Bishop was relatively uncomplicated. When the current Bishop had accomplished the feat of offending 72.6% of the ward it was deemed time to pick a new Bishop. In Utah, the process involved much prayer and fasting, however in Wyoming it went something like this.

The Stake President would show up unannounced to Priesthood Meeting. He would excuse any men who had already been Bishop, (except in Wheatland where there were only 4 available brothers, they had to take turns and just rotated). He then asked the brothers to line up in the cultural hall, remove their jackets, and face the wall. He then methodically walked up and down the line pondering which brother would be the new Bishop. When he was satisfied he asked the brethren to turn around and then he named the new Bishop. (In Utah we have to get authorization from Salt Lake, but in outlying areas the size of the pond needs to be considered.)

For decades it was a mystery why the men were told to turn around, but a former Stake President explained how the process worked. The men were turned around and coats removed so that the President could look at their rear pants pocket and judge the relative prominence of the ring worn by their can of Skoal tobacco. On the surface it would appear to be a straightforward process, but much judgment and experience was required to determine if a "light ring" was from an occasional user or someone whose wife had just bought him a new pair of pants.

The new Bishop obviously would be the brother with the lightest ring. Grant had the good (or bad), fortune of being the only man in his ward that didn't chew, so after the President ruled out the new pants complication, he was called and sustained as the new Bishop.

Until Grant settled in Wyoming our family had seldom hunted out of state, but with his new home and connections, we now had an insider who could find us new hunting grounds. When I was Bishop the only fringe benefit I ever had was one year I got the Ward Choir to sing my favorite Christmas song, "Oh Holy Night," during the Christmas program. Grant did way better than this when he found out that his Counselor, Shane, was originally from Star Valley and had grown up hunting deer in some of the best country in the West.

With Shane guiding and providing horses, we planned a trophy hunt into the fabled Grey's River Mountains east of Star Valley. As the opening of the deer hunt approached a major complication developed. Shane said he could not go with us. I forget his excuse but I think it involved something about his wife having a baby or some such nonsense.

Our hunt plans had long ago passed the point of no return, so we defaulted to the next best option which was purchasing a map. There is nothing unmanly about purchasing a map. In fact, in most hunting circles the ability to read a topographical map is considered a necessary survival skill.

After purchasing the map there arose some discussion regarding the next step, which involved having Shane mark the best routes, trails and hunting areas. The purists among us viewed Shane's marking of the map as akin to "asking directions," and as such to be wholly unbecoming to a real man. The other view was held that in this special incident the information would be accepted but not spoken of ever again. The second viewpoint prevailed and all was well until we unfolded the map and saw a circle drawn around about 500 acres and the word "GRIZZLIES" printed across it in big block letters.

Opening morning found us hiking up the east face of Redtop with the thrill of exploring new county and imagining some of the places we were discovering to be untouched by white men. "Imagining" was the operative word due to the empty beer cans and Snickers wrappers discovered along the trails.

The morning was spent doing more "discovering" than hunting, but it was none the less enjoyable. We saw a few deer but nothing to shoot at, except Jared, who decided that taking a two point three miles and 3,000 vertical feet from camp was fully justifiable. Luckily, he missed. The afternoon was not much better, but we stuck with it until late in the day. We had split up earlier and would probably not see each other until evening in camp.

Dusk found me a little far from camp. I started hustling so as not to be in totally unfamiliar country in the dark. I was about a mile from camp coming down a thick pine covered ridge when I heard something ahead of me. When you are deer hunting and you hear a noise your mind instinctively defaults to "it's a deer." I started sneaking to where the sound came from, with it getting darker by the minute. The next sound I heard was definitely not a deer but a bear tearing up something and woofing. I was now about 30 yards away and curiosity was pulling me closer.

Two thoughts crossed my mind at relatively the same time. As any woman can tell you men cannot multitask, so while these thoughts were not at the same time they were close. The first was that it was now too dark to shoot or even really get a good look at the bear. The second, even more important, was a visualization of the map with the word "GRIZZLIES" in big block letters and the recognition that I was well within the circle.

My gun of choice that day was a 243, which some consider marginal for even deer. If it was indeed a grizzly and I shot in self-defense, it would have only made him mad. They say that what doesn't kill you makes you stronger, except when dealing with bears, they just make you dead. I told myself that if I backed up thirty yards and went down the next ridge over I would get to camp a little sooner. I am glad that I was nearing middle age when this happened, for if I was younger I probably would have had to "see the elephant".

The first year's hunt on Redtop ended with an appreciation of the new country but no deer. As we were packing up for home a group of hunters stopped and asked if they could use our camp spot. They were from Logan, Utah and were looking for a new place to hunt. We said "sure, we are leaving", and then pointed out our favorite areas where we saw the most deer.

As we were planning for the hunt on Redtop the next year I happened to mention to a work associate where we were going. He said that his cousin was a game warden in the area and asked me to say "hi" if we ran into him. I remember thinking, "sure, like I will ever see him."

The day before the hunt we arrived at our camp spot only to find that the men from Logan, which we had helped out last year, were in it. We grumbled a little, but there were other spots we could use. The next morning we woke to about six inches of fresh snow on the ground. It was still dark when we headed up the mountain to our favorite spot, only to run across fresh tracks made by two men. At his point I didn't even have to guess who made them. They took our camp spot and were now going up to hunt our area.

We were nearing the spot we wanted to be at daylight when we heard shots about 400 yards above us on the ridge. Two men were shooting. They emptied their guns, reloaded and emptied them again. We had about 100 yards to get to the crest of our ridge to where we could see into the next valley where the shooting was coming from.

My son Clint was young and more motivated, so he beat the rest of us by a few minutes. I knew I would not get into shooting position in time and, if I did, my breathing would make my poor shooting even worse, so I got out the binoculars and spotted.

The other hunters were out of sight and had quit shooting when I spotted the deer running down the opposite side of the canyon at about 350 yards. They were both big bucks and were untouched by the Logan artillery. Clint threw himself prone on the snow and fired one shot. The back deer dropped, got up and before Clint could shoot again was into the pines.

I was certain that he had made a good shot and we would find the deer just inside the trees. We had a steep hike down the canyon and up the other side. While hiking up the far side we were surprised to see our Logan buddies running down the mountain to the place where the deer had entered the trees. The deer was dead right where we thought it would be, but they beat us to it by a few minutes and had their tag on it by the time we arrived.

I back tracked to where Clint had shot it and showed them that there was no blood on the snow before Clint's shot, but this did no good. It was a great 9X6 nontypical, about 28 inches wide, but we would have to fight to claim it.

While I was thinking bad thoughts about people from Logan, Clint decided that he would try tracking the second buck in the fresh snow. I headed back to pick up some gear from where he had shot. As I was loading up I noticed someone hiking up the trail below us. Something about him didn't seem quite right but it was several minutes before I decided what it was. He was not carrying a rifle.

Why would someone be knee deep in snow, 3,000 feet up a mountain on the opening of deer hunting without a rifle? He was heading toward me and eventually I saw that he was a Game and Fish officer. In Utah they seldom get more than 50 yards from their pickup, so this was something new to me. He was all business, wanting to see my license and wanting to know about all the shooting. I pointed him towards the Loganites, secretly hoping that they had incorrectly tagged OUR deer.

As he left I called out, "your name wouldn't be Hyde would it?" He said yes and I replied, "Your cousin Blaine from Utah says hello." He grunted something turned around and left.

Later at camp Clint told the story of how he tracked the second buck most of the day, finally jumping and shooting him. It was a great 5X5 about 30" wide. By being the bigger man and letting the other hunter take his first deer, Clint ultimately got the opportunity to shoot two world class bucks in one day.

CHAPTER 12

GOOD SHOTS - BAD SHOTS

When hunters gather around the campfire, their exploits (and lies) often revolve around the relative skill they have exhibited with their weapon of choice. Most men believe that deep inside they are one of the few "good shots." My lifetime of hunting experiences has been peppered with season ending "good shots," or season extending "bad shots". Good shots and bad shots are really not as black and white as it would appear, for a bad shot might not be a miss and a good shot might just be luck. Following are a few of the campfire stories and other memories of hunts gone by that examine the subject of good shots and bad shots.

GOOD SHOT: As Reese pulled up to a lookout near the rim of Wildcat, a string of deer were running across a clearing from east to west at about 275 yards. I was riding shotgun and a few other relatives were in the bed.   Reese stepped out and used the hood of the truck as a rest. I exited the passenger door, got my binoculars focused, and announced that there was a buck and, as usual, it was the last deer in the group. As soon as I identified the gender of the deer there were two shots that were so close together as to sound as one. I knew the one came from Reese and the other came from about twelve inches directly over my head.   An unnamed relative had stood up in the bed of the truck and unleashed an offhand shot that permanently damaged my hearing.   The damage eventually was limited to the frequency somewhere near that of my wife's voice. With my ears ringing I watched the deer tumble end over end and not get up.

The shot that dropped the deer was a "good shot" that bordered on being a "great shot."   Reese was shooting a Sako 7MM Mag. that he practiced with regularly. He is probably one of the best rifle shots that I have ever known.   The relative was shooting a borrowed 30-30 with open sights and to my knowledge had not hit a deer in twenty years. I turned to Reese and said, "Good shot." The relative said, "Let's wait on handing out congratulations until we see whose bullet is in the deer."

BAD SHOT: I heard of men excitedly levering out all the shells in their magazine without taking a shot, but really didn't believe it until one day I did a variation of it. A deer was in and out of the brush offering fleeting opportunities for shots. After the deer was dead I went to pick up my brass and found two unfired shells. As near as I can figure, after I shot I would unconsciously lever another round in the chamber, but when the deer stepped into the brush I would have time to wonder if my I had an empty in the chamber so I would rack another one in and the live round that was already in the chamber went to the ground.

GOOD SHOT: Larry and I were at the head of the Big Draw late one morning when we spotted a buck across the gully at about 200 yards. It was Larry's turn, so he unleashed one from his Savage 308. (It was Larry's turn because I was occupied relieving myself from being too hydrated.) I called a miss that was just low. He settled down and shot again.....a hit. The deer didn't move, so he shot again. The Savage held five shots in the rotary magazine and he used them all. As I was handing him my gun to shoot, and taking his to reload, the deer tipped over.

The autopsy concluded that after the first miss Larry had hit the deer three times in the chest in a group that you could cover with your hand, and one shot that went between the buck's legs. We don't know which one killed him but we do know which shot "dropped" him. The mystery of the buck not falling over was solved when Larry mentioned that he had been too cheap to buy deer loads and instead used his 180 grain elk loads, which didn't expand sufficiently.

BAD/NO SHOT: The shot that haunts me most is the one that never happened. Jared and I were near the end of our hike in the Sabille unit of Wyoming. We had spotted two monster bucks lying in the shade of some rim rock. We sneaked to within about 250 yards and set up for the shot. He would take the one on the right and I would take the one on the left. He had his dead in the crosshairs and was waiting for me to get on target. We were standing on our tiptoes leaning over a cliff and for some reason I just couldn't get in a position to shoot. As I finally got settled in, the wind shifted and both deer bolted. Before we could shoot they were over the hill. If I hadn't been greedy and just let

Jared shoot when he was ready he would have a trophy and I could sleep better.

GOOD SHOT? I dropped the guys off at the top of the west dugway near the north end of the radio tower basin. They would push north until they got into the cedars and then go west until they reached George's camp or found me in the truck. When they got to the truck Gordon informed us that he had shot a nice buck. Nice buck is code for a two point. He directed the recovery effort and in short order we were at his prize.

As we were admiring the nice buck someone asked him where he had hit it. His hand searched the chest area and did not come up with a hole. He got somewhat nervous and intensified the quest for a bullet hole. About this time Bob Hansen noticed that the deer was blind in one eye. As we were dragging the deer back to the truck the following comment was heard, "I don't think you even hit him, you must have just scared him and since he is blind, he probably ran into a tree and broke his neck". To this day Gordy maintains that he did shoot the deer, but a hole was never found.

GOOD SHOT: It was the last day of the hunt and Cousin Lee and I still had deer tags in our pockets. It had been an unproductive day, but as dusk was settling in we made one last drive going west by the low road. We had just passed the canyon where Dad had his second heart attack, but were not quite to the place where Grant once shot the deer that Larry had hit first. A group of about eight deer came out of the brush heading north. They were running straight away from us when I spied horns on the last one. It was an Eastern two point, but since we were in the West some would call it a spike.

It was at about 175 yards still moving away when I threw my 25-06 up and took an offhand shot. This however was not just any offhand shot but one that couldn't miss. Since I did not want to take a Texas heart shot (slang for rear end shots), the crosshairs seem to almost magically rest on the back of the deer's head. As I sent the slug on its way I was in no way surprised when the deer skidded to a stop and only next moved when I threw him in the bed of the truck. By the time we got him loaded up I noticed that he only had one antler. The other side and some of his skull were missing. Several years later while hiking in the general area I found the other horn and skull plate bleached white.

OK SHOT/GOOD SHOT: A few years after making the above "good" head shot I found myself in almost the same situation. I was on top of the oak brush side hill heading toward the Grassy Knoll. I could see a buck 200 yards ahead of me in the brush and he was not going to move. If he did move he would go deeper in the brush and I would have no shot. He was looking directly away from me so once again I was looking at an undesirable shot.

With the confidence of a hunter that had made a string of "one in a row" head shots, I decided that this situation called for the same shot. I didn't have anything to rest on so once again the crosshairs settled on the back of his head and with an offhand shot I dropped him like a sack of potatoes.

When I had hiked about halfway to my prize he stood up, wheeled around, and was gone into the brush. About fifteen seconds later I heard a shot that was not too far away. I located the spot where the deer was standing when I shot at him. There was no blood, just one of his antlers from about an inch above the skull.

When you shoot a deer's antler off it usually knocks him cold for a short period of time, but as soon as he comes to his senses he acts like nothing ever happened. Once the deer decided that he was not permanently incapacitated he ran a couple of hundred yards right into Gordon. Gordon looked through his scope and commented, "That deer has only one antler" and shot him dead. This deer with only one antler was actually quite an improvement for Gordy because his last one had only one eye.

GOOD SHOT/BAD SHOT: G---T watched a line of deer sneak up the gully on the Strawberry side. The fourth one back was a nice buck. As soon the deer cleared a lone cedar tree they would be in the open. As they cleared the tree he counted the deer off.....one, two, three, four, BANG. The fourth deer dropped, a "good shot".

In a previous epistle the story was told of a deer that had one antler shot off and the other hidden under a sagebrush, giving the hunter a moment of anguish. In this case the anguish was of a more permanent nature because there was no hidden antler...or antlers...a doe!! There is no doubt that the real buck lived to a ripe old age since he was smart enough to trade places in line with an unsuspecting doe. There were few secrets in deer camp but Dad never knew about G---T's doe killing.

A variation of this "smart" deer phenomenon that also applies to ducks was explained to me by Grandpa Colledge. He would never place an even dozen decoys out because the smarter ducks could count to twelve, know that it was trap, and veer off.

BAD SHOT/GOOD SHOT: I peeked off of the north overlook on the west side of the Big Draw. The deer must have already heard me because they were flat out running. I was young, confident, and had my trusty 243, so the fact that it was only 350 yards didn't dissuade me from lying down, picking out the three point buck, taking the shot, and watching the deer drop. Boy, it was a "good" shot. It was a "good" shot right up to the point that the deer stood up and took off into the cedars, changing it immediately into a "bad" shot. I tracked the deer most of the afternoon until I ran out of blood and tracks. I could tell that he was hit in the left rear. Somewhere in the second hour of tracking I reevaluated my skill level and future choices in shot selection.

Two weeks later, and two miles to the east, Bob and I were sneaking to within muzzle loader range of another three point that we had spotted. We both shot at about the same time and when the smoke cleared the buck was down.   The foray was well planned except the part where we forgot to shoot the deer uphill from the truck instead of downhill in the brush-choked gully where he died. When we finally got the deer back to the road a post mortem revealed he had a hole in his left rear ham that was almost healed. This was the same deer I had hit two weeks before.

GOOD SHOT/BAD SHOT: My son Eric had drawn a coveted moose tag. We had seen a few good moose but not any great ones. Time was running short so we decided to sneak up on one of the GOOD ones. I had the moose in the spotting scope and would stay on the ridge while Eric and his brother Jared got within rifle range. While they were closing the distance I happened to glass an adjacent hill. Wow, I had found a GREAT moose but Eric was about to shoot the smaller one. I got their attention seconds before he pulled the trigger. Our focus was now on this new trophy. I once again looked through the spotting scope while they got into position and fired. At the shot the moose totally collapsed. I have seen a few moose shot but had never seen one drop like this.

When I worked my way to the boys I mentioned that the moose looked like he had been head shot. Eric assured me that the crosshairs were on his chest when he shot. When we got to the moose the bullet hole was in his forehead. It was determined that Eric, who was using my gun, had placed the wrong horizontal scope wire on the moose and shot two feet high.

BAD SHOT/SECOND CHANCE SHOT: The following is told by Brother Larry.

At a young age I realized that I liked to hunt a little different than the others. I didn't really need optics and I didn't want to sit and glass the mountain, I wanted to hike through the hills and jump shoot the deer. To the best of my recollection, 5 of the first 6 deer that I shot were on the move. Also, my legs were very short and there was no way in the world that I could win a race to the Big Draw. Lee, Brian and Jeff were just too fast.

Once the truck hit the summit of the mountain I was the first to jump out and headed east, the total opposite direction than the rest of the party. I like to hike slow and just enjoy the experience, but don't get me wrong; getting the buck was still the most important thing. Without a buck I would have to spend the next year being only half a man. I saw the effect it had on Jeff, and it wasn't pretty.

I remember it being the opening morning of the hunt when I was 18 or 19. As I got out of the truck to do my usual hike, Uncle Bert asked me if it was ok if he came along. I always went alone so I was a little surprised. Of course I quickly answered in the affirmative because Uncle Bert was great company. When I took off on this hunt, I never caught the truck back to the cabin, so this usually ended up to be a good 5+ mile hike. Uncle Bert talked to Dad and asked him to pick him up at the Square Pines. I guess he figured that 2 miles with me was better than 6 miles.

We hiked along the ridge through the head of the first canyon; the next area was my secret spot. I had got a buck out of it the year before and I knew right where to go. The area consisted of a couple of small patches of quakies that connected to a bigger patch. Two weeks earlier these quakies were in their full autumn glory, but now the leaves had all fallen to the ground and, as my boy Colton once said, it looked like the ground was littered with gold dollars.

As we skirted along the quakies, a few deer came out of the bottom about 100 yards away. Seeing a "nice" 2 point I brought up my 308 Savage, hurriedly looked down the open sighted barrel and took a quick snap shot. After all, I wanted to beat Uncle Bert to the punch. I did get off the first shot, but the buck was untouched. Thinking I would hear a shot and watch the deer drop at any second I only heard Uncle Bert say, "take your time and make your shot count." A few seconds later I shot again and dropped the buck. "Why didn't you shoot," I asked Uncle Bert," did your gun jam?" "No," he explained, "I just wanted to watch you shoot your deer."

The concept of letting someone else get the buck was totally foreign to me. As Uncle Bert advanced to favorite uncle status I was still confused as to how this could all happen. Years later with kids of my own I realized that the deer hunt is a lot more than just shooting a deer.

CHAPTER 13

GUN LUST

My brother Gordy said that after having two daughters and then a boy he was worried that his heir to the throne might be unduly influenced in the feminine way. His fears were laid to rest when one day while the girls were playing dolls his son Alex picked up a Barbie, bent her at the waist to ninety degrees and proceeded to shoot the TV with his Barbie.

If only he had a pistol.

I am not sure where it all began for me, but I definitely remember having a pair of cap pistols. They were pearl handled, nickel-plated genuine plastic. They shot real caps that you bought in boxes of five. The rolls of caps were still attached to each other and it took an experienced cowboy to separate the individual rolls without crushing them so they would feed correctly.

If only I had a "BB" gun.

My first real gun was, of course, a Daisy air rifle. This sounded so much more lethal than just a "BB gun." The single cock lever action held about 400 BB's, so you only had to reload about every hour or so. Campbell's soup cans, which we pretended were Indians, were placed in a row on the top rail of the backyard fence and knocked off before they could get an arrow into us.

One day after the Indians had been dispatched, I ventured to the row of trees north of our pasture. There were several starlings about 50 feet up mocking me. I took carful aim and a .177 caliber BB was launched from my smoothbore air rifle. The starlings still laughed. After expending about one fourth of my magazine (100), I came to the conclusion that the birds were either bullet, I mean BB proof, or that they were out of range. Another possibility was that I was just missing, but this option really never crossed my mind.

If only I had a pellet gun.

The two pellet gun religions were Benjamin and Sheridan. I was converted and baptized into the Benjamin fold. My pellet gun was a multi pump, single shot, of the .117 caliber persuasion. .22 caliber versions were available, but they lacked the flexibility of shooting both lead pellets and normal BB's. Real pellets came in a green metal can with a screw-on lid. We learned not to keep them in our back pocket to avoid adults inspecting us for a can of Skoal.

Pellets were expensive and saved for small game, not just target shooting. If someone is mentally a little slow it is fashionable to blame it on lead poisoning from paint, however in our case it is from having a spare pellet at the ready in our mouth for most of the summer.

The instructions stated that you pumped the gun from one to ten times depending on the power level you desired. We only used one or ten pumps, the former to shoot your brother in the rear end and the latter to slay birds. Of course within the first week we tried 50 pumps thinking it would probably take down a deer. Ten pumps was realistically the practical limit, but we usually did twelve just to be sure.

Like a muzzleloader, the Benjamin was a single shot and nothing prevented you from loading multiple BB's. We experimented with this concept but settled on the inherent accuracy of just the single projectile. We now possessed a firearm, or airarm, that was accurate out to 100 feet or so.

The factory sights were the limiting factor, so through an ad in Boys Life we ordered a "peep" sight. In the quest for even more accuracy we ordered the "fine" aperture for the peep, thinking that this would increase the odds of a more consistent sight picture. We soon learned that all the fine peep did was made it harder to see the intended target. The pellet gun served us well but was marginal on rabbits and squirrels.

If only I had a .22.

I learned on Mom's .22 that she got as a wedding present (why don't we do that anymore)? It was a Marlin bolt action with a full-size stock. It was the most accurate .22 I have ever used, but its dimensions were more suited for a six footer than a ten year old of unusually small stature (I wrestled 88 pounds in high school).

Upon earning my Eagle Scout rank, Dad bought me a Winchester semi auto model 290. I still have that .22, and between my four younger brothers, six sons, daughter, and several neighbor kids, it has had about 2 million rounds through it. A .22 was great for land-based small game but made shooting pheasants on the fly challenging, if not illegal.

If only I had a shotgun.

While living on the ranch I used the 410 my dad received while growing up in Mammoth. It was a Winchester single shot that made an extremely safe learner's gun because the hammer took both hands to pull back if you were anyone other than a professional wrestler. As a sporting arm the 410 left much to be desired, and I have since determined that the sole reason for its creation was to make the sport of shooting clay pigeons very difficult.

In preparation for the duck hunt of 1966 I received my first shotgun. It was Stevens single shot in 16 gauge with a unique side lever for breaking the action. The 16 gauge was invented to have the kick of a 12 gauge with the shot charge of a 20 gauge.

On the first Saturday in October, Dad and I picked up Grandpa Colledge and headed for the Jordan River west of Lehi. We selected a spot that offered a small amount of concealment, hunkered down and waited for the first flock to appear. For some unexplained reason the opening of duck season begins at noon on the first day but at daylight thereafter. Everyone's watch seemed to be about five minutes fast on the opening day so we prepared for battle.

We saw a flock of five or six mallards zigzagging toward our location. Just when I thought they would zag away from us Grandpa blew his call, they made an abrupt turn and then came directly over us. In the ensuing volley two ducks fell and Grandpa said one of them was mine. When I hunt with my grandkids I will make sure they "dropped" whatever they shoot at.

When we were old enough to drive we spent a lot of time at Powell's Slough. Brother Larry and the Footes would accompany me duck hunting in my hunting rig ('61 Mercury Comet). The inherent flaw of having only one shot soon became apparent while dozens of blue wing teal laughed at us while rocketing by at 60 MPH.

About this time Dad stopped duck hunting, so I confiscated his twelve gauge Browning semi-auto model A5 and used it for several years. Dad surprised us one opening day in Logan by showing up and wanting his Browning back. I dusted off the 16 gauge and was reacquainted with its limitations.

If I only had a semi-automatic twelve gauge shotgun.

Later in life, quite by accident, I picked an Ithaca semi-auto twelve gauge at the gun counter at Wolfe's Sporting Goods. It just felt good. I could visualize the ducks and pheasants dropping like flies. I somehow convinced my new bride of the wisdom of purchasing the gun to provide food for the new family we were starting.

Dad occasionally let me take a shot with Mom's Marlin 30-30. It must have been defective since I missed several deer. It was a great gun to keep behind the seat of the pickup, but how could I be expected to kill deer with an unfamiliar gun.

If only I had my own deer rifle.

The Christmas of my sixteenth year was memorable because of the long and narrow box under the tree. It was a Savage 99F in 308. The Savage had a rotary magazine that held five rounds and its gold trigger signified the Model "F" for featherweight. I think it weighed four ounces less than the normal rifle but did kick about twice as much.

The reason for this rifle selection was that when dad came back from WWII he bought the most powerful lever action available. It was a Savage model 99. He batted right but was left handed in writing and shooting. There were very few left handed bolt action rifles so a lever gun was chosen. The Savage worked for him so he, or Santa, brought me one. For hunting the thick brush or a quick follow up shot the Savage excelled. I loved that gun for elk but was eventually persuaded to follow the smaller-projectile-at-a-faster-velocity club for deer. How can a man be expected to use the same gun for both species?

If only I had a bolt action 25-06.

The siren song of Wolfe's gun counter called and I answered. The call took the form of a Remington Model 700. I was now in possession of the very tool needed to provide venison for my growing family. We became best friends and she never let me down. The best shots I have ever made were with that gun. I have killed more deer with it than all the rest of my rifles put together. If I ever had to own only one gun (I just shuddered), it would be this very rifle. It would sure be nice to have a small gun that didn't kick very much for my wife to use. Her birthday was coming up soon.

If only she had a 243.

I picked up the 243 Remington 788 at a yard sale. With proper reloading it could be used for both deer and varmints. Many a rabbit came to a screeching stop at the request of the 243. Due to a factory defect (I got a reload too hot and broke the stuck bolt off with a rock), the barrel was replaced with a shorter 18 inch version. I then cut the stock down and now had the perfect kid starter rifle. It was roughly the same size as a Ruger .22 and didn't kick much more. All seven of my children, most of my nieces and nephews, some friends, and even a few strangers have learned to shoot with this gun. Someday I might need to branch out to antelope hunting and I didn't even have the appropriate rifle for it.

If only I had a 257 Weatherby.

The Weatherby came about due to a few trades. Not gun for gun, but furnace parts for gun parts. While installing heating ducts in the basement of a friend I learned that he fabricated gun barrels. A trade was agreed upon and he asked me what I wanted. A 257 Weatherby sounded exotic, fast, and deadly. I knew a salesman on the previously mentioned Wolf's gun counter who had a Sako action and then traded Cousin Danny a furnace for a stock and his gunsmithing abilities to put it all together. This is still my most accurate rifle. Out to 700 yards it will make any animal DRT (dead right there). I still NEEDED a few guns.

If only I had a _____.

You get the idea? There arose the need and then the justification for a 22-250, 7MM Rem Mag, 7MM STW, 7MM WSM, 300 Win Mag, etc. not to speak of the pistols and muzzle loaders. There was one final gun to purchase. There is really no need or justification for it other that I just wanted it, so I waited until they were hard to get, extremely expensive, and then bought one. A Bushmaster AR15 in .223.

I tell myself that I have enough guns. **But if my wife won't listen to me why should I?**

CHAPTER 14

DECEPTION

Hunters are not born deceptive, but the Darwinian theory of natural selection inherently rewards them for this behavior. Very early they learn that if the deer are on the north side of the mountain their odds of eating venison increase if other hunters migrate to the south side. I am sure that my ancestors exhibited this character flaw for generations, but the first one that I personally knew was my Grandpa Colledge.

Grandpa gained the reputation of being a "serious deer hunter" long before it was fashionable. A few weeks before deer season began, men were known to seek his advice on where to hunt to find a good deer. If indoors, he would direct the inquiring party to go outside and find a patch of dirt. He would smooth out about four square feet of ground with his hand so he could draw a map with a stick. A true outdoorsman never knelt while drawing, but "hunkered." Hunkering is a refined version of the "squat," and more befitting of a man of the mountains.

He would usually start the map in Lehi and end with an "X" marking the secret hunting location. The directions and instructions were usually accompanied by camping advice and tales of past successful forays. My dad told me of watching Grandpa going through the map ritual and being quite impressed that he would tell sometimes complete strangers where his hunting spots were. After listening to the whole conversation he observed that although the directions were accurate and clear, the destination with the "X" on it was anywhere from 25 to 50 miles from anywhere grandpa had ever hunted.

Cousin Jay was the closest thing I have had to a big brother. He was three or four years older than me when he came to stay with us at the ranch one summer. I was accustomed to being the oldest, so it took a little adjusting to not being in charge. I soon learned to enjoy the new family dynamic as he was now expected to do the majority of the heavy lifting around the ranch. He taught me a few things with the following being one of the more memorable.

There was a problem. Jay had spotted a nice buck east of the side hill, but so had another group of hunters. Both Jay and the interlopers shot at approximately the same time and the deer disappeared into the oak brush. As both parties searched the last known location of the deer Larry and I watched to see who would claim the prize. Shortly after entering the thick brush, Jay shouted at the top of his lungs "I got it." Now that ownership had been established the other hunters dejectedly left.

We hiked to where Jay was to help him pack the deer out. When we approached his first words were not ones of delight but the question, "have the other guys left yet?" Once we assured him that they were gone he admitted that in his opinion he had indeed "GOT" the deer, but had not actually "FOUND" the deer. He just needed a little time without the other hunters getting in his way to locate the downed animal. We spread out and soon picked up the trail. A short time later Jay was able to place his tag on the deer that he had obtained by almost fair and square means.

The morning hunt had been uneventful so we were on our way down the mountain to get lunch. We were almost to the Square Pines when we saw Reese driving toward us. As his truck neared ours he slammed on the brakes and jumped out of the cab with rifle in hand. He looked into the bottom of a very steep canyon that stretched below us and quickly took a shot. After the shot he excitedly started jumping up and down hollering "I got him, I got him."

I was watching the whole show and had never even seen the deer. As I was starting to question my sight and deer finding skills he said "Help me go down and drag the deer up to the truck." The deer was at least 300 yards away, almost straight downhill and in some of the thickest oak brush on the mountain. Reese was a known practical joker, so I quizzed him to discern if he had really shot a deer. He assured me on all that was Holy that he had indeed shot a deer, and if I was a real friend I would help him get it out of the hell hole where it was located. I reasoned that if he was willing to go down the canyon with me he indeed must have a deer there.

We swam through the brush and eventually found the deer close to where he had shot. The deer was propped up in the brush and already gutted. He had shot it first thing in the morning and was on his way to retrieve it when I drove into view. His shooting and theatrics were to enroll me into his scheme of retrieving the deer with the least amount of expended energy (his energy).

A close second cousin to Deception is Mr. Annoyance. I was introduced to him at a young age while going up the mountain with my Dad. It was late afternoon and we were on our way to the top of the mountain for the evening hunt. About half way to our destination we caught up with a local truck going up the dirt trail at two miles per hour. Road hunting was a long established local pastime that the occupants were enjoying to the fullest. In my naive mind I thought that they would pull over at the first wide spot in the road. WRONG!

When they did not pull over I assumed that they were so engrossed in looking for deer that they had not noticed us. About 400 yards later this assumption was proven false as I definitely saw the driver look at us in his mirror. Dad lightly tapped his horn, but they acted as if they had heard nothing. Seeing that they were hearing impaired, Dad leaned on the horn a little longer. I was fairly young and thought that the driver was sticking his arm out the window to wave us around them, but I now remember that I didn't see him use all of his fingers.

Dad was a calm person up to a point, but that point had passed several minutes ago. He uttered a few words that were ones I had promised in the Deer Hunter's Oath not to not tell Mom about, hit the accelerator and lurched into the sagebrush on the side of the road. With brush and dirt flying he bounced our truck by the side of the offender, calmly asked the driver not to be so rude in the future, cut back in front of him and missed his front bumper by at least half an inch. We then drove to our evening hunting spot but I don't remember if we saw any deer.

Deception is usually practiced by hunters, not the hunted, but Gordon and Cousin Cole found a deer that was well versed in the art. As they hunted along Current Creek a buck jumped from cover and tried to elude them. Gordy made a great running shot as the deer disappeared into the thick brush (the deer was running, not Gord). They quickly picked up the trail of the elusive buck and followed as it weaved in and out of the cover in its efforts to escape. The tracks came to a sudden stop at the edge of a twenty foot cliff that dropped into the creek. No deer could possibly survive that fall, but there was nowhere else it could have gone. The only option that didn't involve jumping off cliffs or getting wet was for the hunters to hike a half mile to the east where there was a bridge. Once safely over the creek, they hiked a half mile back upstream until they had reached the spot that was straight across from the cliff that the deer had apparently jumped off. The deer must have read Louis L'Amour novels because, just as outlaws would have done, he went up the creek to avoid being tracked. Cole and Gordon had also read the novels, so they knew they had to go upstream and look for the place he exited. They found where the deer had left the stream and apparently after a few more evasive maneuvers, had run out of blood, which ended his escape.

The most coveted deer tag in the world is the Henry Mountains. In college about 1972, I took statistics, but had not had the opportunity to use the knowledge gained in that college class until calculating my odds of drawing that hunt. The numbers didn't lie. I was guaranteed to draw the tag sometime within the next 72 years. Since I didn't think I could make it to the year 2085 I looked at other options. One that intrigued me was the Henrys Management Hunt. This hunt allows the recipient the opportunity to take any buck he wants, as long as it only has three points or less on one side. I had enough points to obtain this tag, so I started planning.

After several scouting trips I found a management deer that I would be proud to cull out of the herd. He was a heavy, symmetrical, 32 inch, 3X3. I had seen him on two different occasions near the same canyon, and a one mile hike from the trailhead would bring us to the 3X3's lair.

As we drove in the dark on opening morning we were stopped about a mile short of our destination by the Fish and Game. There have been a few times in my life (well, maybe more than a few) when the sight of the Fish Cops made me nervous, but today I had all the correct paperwork. After he determined that I had violated no game laws he asked me where I was going to hunt. (No, this is not the part of the story where the subject of deception is discussed.) When I informed him of my destination he chuckled. He had just come from that trailhead and said that there were at least fifteen trucks parked there.

With my plans dashed I picked a less desirable location. The morning hunt was uneventful, but I did hear shooting near the canyon my three point called home. Before going to camp for lunch I decided to go to the trailhead to see if they had shot my deer. To my surprise, one of the camp followers was a man that I had worked with many years ago. He told the following story.

Their hunter had spotted a nice deer while scouting in the fall, but it was not MY deer. It was located in the canyon adjacent to the one I wanted to hunt. They were unsure if their deer would be in the same location, so to increase their odds they would create the illusion of a dozen people hunting this area which would drive any competition (ME) away. They actually drove most of the vehicles to the trailhead the night before so as not to miss the very early risers. Fifteen trucks and only one hunter, BRILLIANT!

They got their deer (which was not as big as the one I was looking for) on the opening morning, so I started hunting my canyon the next day. I never again saw the deer I had originally scouted. All the commotion must have driven it into the next county. I did shoot a nice 30 inch 3X4, but it was three miles and 1,000 feet below the trailhead. Luckily I had Dave Told and Jim Brisk to help pack it out. I only wish they would have remembered their backpacks and were not almost as old as I was.

CHAPTER 15

IT'S JUST NOT FAIR

One day Cousin Tom accidently combined the art of road hunting, a close shot, and a dose of laziness to create an unbeatable package that was so good that it did not even require deception. He was supposed to be at camp early in the morning to go up the mountain with us. When he didn't show up at the designated time we did what all hunters do: waited two minutes and left him. About eleven o'clock in the morning I had given up hope of seeing a deer when I heard a truck coming up the road below me. I had hiked all morning through the brush and had been sitting down taking a break. The truck stopped and out stepped Tom. I thought "Great, at least I can get a ride down the mountain," but instead of hollering at me he pulled out his rifle and shot a four point that was right below me. I had been within 200 yards of the deer for the last half an hour but the noise of the truck scared it into revealing its location to the late arrivals. What I learned from Tom was that it paid to sleep in, eat breakfast at Chick's in Heber, sashay up the mountain, shoot the deer, and then ask me to help drag it to the truck.

IT'S JUST NOT FAIR

During the first few years of muzzle loading Larry was somewhat jinxed. While he participated in several group kills, he was unable to get a buck on his own. One morning we were riding to the Big Draw, and right as we got out to start hiking, a group of deer took off at a dead run, the last one being a nice buck. Everyone missed except Larry, who calmly dropped it. It was hit hard but managed to get back up and into the brush. Larry was excited because a deer hit like that will go a short distance and lie down and die or will be easy to sneak up on and finish.

This was very open country, so we surrounded the deer to make sure it did not get away. The deer exited nearest to Brother Grant and after he missed, reloaded and shot again the deer dropped from an uncalled head shot. Larry was sure that his deer would have only gone a short way before expiring but according to camp rules it was now Grant's deer.

IT'S JUST NOT FAIR

My sons Logan and Kevin were fourteen and twelve, respectively. We had planned to go to Fishlake to try and shoot their deer, but the weather would not be pleasant at 11,500 feet so we decided to try Wildcat. The night before the opening we scouted a little but found almost no deer. It was a bad situation. The weather was keeping us from the high country and the deer had not yet moved into the lower winter range.

Just before dark I took one last look through the binoculars. Below an old oil well I could see a few deer and in the fading light I could make out two bucks. One was small 4X6 and the other was a big 3X3 with antlers that looked like a whitetail. The deer were on the west side of a small canyon. If we could sneak to the rim rock on the east side we would have a good shot, providing they didn't move during the night. They were not spooked, so we backed off, with the plan to be on them tomorrow.

In the morning we stopped where an old two track split from the road and led to the rim rock. If anyone drove on this they would scare the deer away. I parked several hundred yards from the canyon and maybe just a little on the two track. If anyone happened along I wanted them to know that they had company. The boys and I stealthy progressed to the rim rock overlook. Tension mounted in direct relationship to the gathering light.

When it became light enough to shoot we were amazed to find that our deer had not moved twenty feet from their location of last night. Since this would be Kevin's first deer I gave him first choice of which one to shoot. He picked the 4X6. As he got set up for the shot older Brother Clint assisted Logan in getting ready to shoot his 3X3. Immediately after Kevin shot, Logan followed. They both connected on perfect lung shots and the deer fell. It was five minutes after the opening and we were done. We had to drive around to the other side of the canyon to retrieve the deer. While hiking to the deer we passed some hunters that had showed up after we had shot. As we dragged the deer past them I heard one of them say

IT'S JUST NOT FAIR

My son Ryan was a teenager and looking for his first deer. He hunted hard and had faithfully put in the time needed for fate to smile on him. In the evening he jumped a buck northeast of Reese's Rock, and as it slowed down he got a good rest, took careful aim, and squeezed the trigger. The deer dropped at the shot but slowly got up and sneaked off.

He found me and his brothers Clint, Jared, Eric, Logan, and Kevin before following the deer. With the family assembled we commenced to have a class in tracking. It grew dark before we found the deer, so being true sportsmen we decided to resume in the morning. The fact that tomorrow was Sunday and the boys would miss church to track the deer had no bearing on their willingness to participate.

Sunday morning found us on the trail of Ryan's deer. I would let the younger boys try to find the tracks or blood and they were getting better by the yard. Two hours after we started we saw a familiar sight about ten yards ahead of us. A gut pile was in the trail that we were following. There were no more tracks to follow only drag marks to the nearest road. Ryan remembered that about ten minutes after he had shot the deer he heard a shot to the west. Some lowlife had shot Ryan's deer, probably just as it was tipping over, and then claimed it.

IT'S JUST NOT FAIR

Our group had hiked for several miles across the top of Sabille Canyon with no results. We met at the east end to decide on what route to take back to camp. It was agreed that Grant and his father-in-law Ken Nickell would push below the rim rock while Jed Hill and I would hike above it. We had been discussing how to judge deer so he would not shoot one that he would later regret. Jed said he would be happy with any four point over 22 inches.

We were going around the head of the first big canyon to the west when we heard hooves on rocks coming in our direction. We were ready when the buck stepped into view. It was a beautiful, heavy four point that was 26 inches wide. Jed turned to me and asked, "Is it big enough to shoot? I might have said something like "Heck yes, SHOOT." I must have rattled Jed because he promptly missed the 100 yard shot. He shot the second time and I couldn't tell if he connected. About now the deer was thinking seriously about moving to the next county while I was thinking it might be time for me to chamber a round before he got away. As I brought my gun up the deer tipped over. I guess his second shot DID connect. As we were inspecting the trophy, Grant and Ken came puffing up the canyon. They said they had jumped the buck as he was bedded in the shade of the rim rock but could not get a shot before he disappeared. They never said the words, but we know they were thinking

IT'S JUST NOT FAIR

Another trip to Sabille found my son Jared sorting through a bunch of pretty good bucks but not shooting because none were quite big enough. He finally saw a large buck with double drop tines. As he got ready for a shot it spooked and disappeared, never to be seen again. It was the last day of his hunt so he dejectedly headed for camp.

Just before reaching camp he spotted a spike by two. It was 350 yards away but he coolly got a rest and announced that he would shoot the deer between the eyes. He shot and when they approached the deer he had indeed hit right where he had called. The deer's skull was broken, the antlers were drooping, and he now had a poor version of a drop tine buck.

IT'S JUST NOT FAIR

Cousin Lee was not feeling well. It was our first trip to the Boulder Mountains, and the night before he had drunk too much of something a little stronger that Grape Nehi. When we left camp opening morning he groaned and told us he would not be participating today.

He crawled out of the tent about five PM and still didn't look too good. I mentioned that I was going to hunt the edge of the trees near the alfalfa field where we were camped. He said that he would try to walk the 300 yards and hunt near me. A half hour after we were positioned I heard a shot from his direction. I walked over to find he had dropped a nice buck. As it turned out Lee had hunted the least of anyone in camp and had shot the only deer on the opening day.

IT'S JUST NOT FAIR

IT'S JUST NOT FAIR exclaimed my favorite daughter Lacy. She is the only girl among her six brothers. At an early age she felt the pain of discrimination because of rule number one in deer camp (no women). She is as good a shot as her brothers. In fact, she would not marry a man she could out-shoot. Luckily, she found a former marine that filled the bill named Kevin.

As she was leaving high school we went to a place that did not have the woman restrictions. The hunting area was near Monticello. Jeff Pyne and daughter Missy agreed to accompany us on this father/daughter outing. We stayed in a motel in town, ate dinner in a restaurant every night, rode around in the truck eating cookies and told ourselves we were roughing it.

We men found that we had missed out on a lot of fun all those years by following rule number one. The girls made great shots (near the road) and bagged their deer. Dad might have helped clean them a little, but were rewarded by learning a new way to hunt.

CHAPTER 16

BOWS-N-ARROWS

In her cupboard Aunt Karen had a large spool of stuff that was somewhere between heavy string and light twine. It was waxed and its sole purpose, as far as my ten year old mind could figure out, was to be used for the string on a set of bow-n-arrows. Bow and arrows was not to be pronounced as three words, but as one long one. When Larry and I went to see Cousin Brian, the first thing we did was to locate the bow string spool and head for their fruit trees to make bows-n-arrows. More discerning archers preferred osage orange or hickory, but we got along just fine with cherry limbs. The bows were plenty springy, but the arrows were so crooked that the effective range was about ten feet. If you ever did really launch an arrow there was a good chance that it would circle around and hit you.

The next step for the young archer was to plead for a real bow for Christmas. After several unsuccessful petitions, Santa came through and we were armed with 25 pound bows and real, if cheap, arrows. Keeping supplied with arrows proved to be more expensive than just worrying about a having a sufficient quantity of BB's. Our supply of arrows would eventually shrink to the critical stage due to having been lost, broken, or confiscated. A trip to town was now required. We lived about 2 miles from downtown Pleasant Grove and the likely, if not preferred, mode of transportation was hopping on our bicycles and riding to town, telling mom not to worry as we peddled off.

Main Street was exactly one block long and the second building on the east side was Radmall's hardware. It was a treasure trove of nuts, bolts, paint, muskrat traps, .22 shells, wrist rockets, and of course, arrows. The arrows were kept in a cutoff cardboard box about six feet up on a shelf behind the counter. We were required to have someone get the box down for us so we could begin the inspection process. When you were expected to pay the unreasonable sum of 25 cents per arrow they had darn well better be straight. After going through the box of approximately 100 arrows and picking out the three straightest, we would pay the clerk and head home.

Summer would occasionally find us in the pasture between our home and the old house to the west of us owned by Aunt Lucille and Uncle Bill. Aunt Lucille and Uncle Bill were actually no relation, but were more like adopted grandparents. We would take our red hooded sweatshirts from the deer hunt, place them on the grass, lay on them, and search the sky to find a cloud that looked like something real. This was good for about five minutes and then our minds turned to something more exciting. We would take our bows-n-arrows, shoot straight up, and watch the arrow fall. We would play chicken and see who would run from the prone position first. This diversion was quite harmless when using bows made of cherry tree limbs, but took on a whole new dimension when shooting 25 to 30 pound bows.

If atmospheric conditions were favorable it was possible to shoot the arrow out of sight. The first time we visually lost an arrow, macho soon turned to panic and we ran like little girls. Our fears were vindicated by watching the falling arrow sink deep into the hood of a red sweatshirt. The motion was made and unanimously ratified to move onto the next level of archery.

We spent considerable time trying to perfect a suitable poison for the sheet metal arrow heads that we fabricated in Dad's shop. The formula usually revolved around whatever we could find in the barn and shop. I remember using soldering flux, dehorning paste, salt, alcohol, coffee grounds, some tobacco from a cigarette butt, some roots and plants that someone said the Indians had once used and were poisonous. Battery acid, if found, was always a good addition, but if you knew a bricklayer, muriatic acid was the ultimate. All of these items were mixed to the proper ratios and then added to the one final component: red powdered sheep dye.

Sheep were not branded like cattle because the wool would be ruined, but they had to be marked somehow. One solution was to make a branding iron that was never heated, but dipped into the very fine red powder and stamped onto the sheep's wool. A side benefit of the red dye was that it made excellent war paint. We spent part of one summer pretending to be Indians, and trying not to be cut by our poisoned arrows.

Upon entering high school, of course we enrolled in shop. The first priority in any shop class was obtaining the training and materials necessary to create some form of weapon. In metal shop the sky was the limit where weapon possibilities were concerned, but somehow we ended up in woodshop. It was our teacher, wise in the ways of young men, who suggested purchasing recurve bow kits. The kits were composed of the necessary parts to glue, laminate, file, sand, and shape a rough version of a 45 pound bow.

I suppose that since the times of the ancients, building your own bow, practicing, and eventually shooting your own food has been a source of filling the need of young males around the world to provide for their tribe and take a necessary step toward manhood. Making mother's requested bookshelf was at least fourteenth or fifteenth down the list in woodshop. As romantic as making your own bow sounded, I broke with tradition and just bought my bow at Park's Sportsman. I had worked most of the summer before school started and had the necessary means to purchase a genuine Shakespeare Super Necedah recurve bow. It was a light brown beauty and did not delaminate in the heat of battle like some of my buddies' shop-made ones.

Evenings before chores would likely find us between the barn and the house shooting into hay bales and trying not to hit the milk cow. If the cow saw us anywhere near the barn after 4 PM, she assumed we were there to milk her and came in from the pasture. Our target was usually a paper plate since it was too hard to get the arrows out of the Zerex can we used to sight-in for the rifle hunt.

About this time one of us was old enough for a driver's license, so a whole new world of adventures opened up. The previous year we had acquired the plans and templates for building kayaks. The process of cutting, gluing, canvassing, and painting kept us busy for most of that summer. With transportation, bows, and kayaks, the next logical step was to go to Utah Lake and shoot carp. Occasionally, the water would be too shallow for the kayaks so we would just walk in the flooded fields in our cut off Levi's and Converse All Stars looking for a ripple that signaled an escaping carp. I don't care how many times it happens, you NEVER get used to a five pound carp unexpectedly brushing against your bare leg.

After proving yourself on carp it was time to move up to big game, meaning deer. None of us had ever bow hunted deer and our familiar hunting ground was void of deer in August, due to it being winter range. An acquaintance offered to show us West Canyon near Cedar Fort. The Friday before the opening we drove up the canyon, crossed the creek and made camp. About dusk a light rain started falling, so we retired to the tents a little early. As the rain increased during the night several leaks manifested themselves. Our feet were on the lower end of the tent and soon we could feel our sleeping bags getting wet. The rain kept up all night and by morning we were curled up into little balls in the top of our bags.

It was still raining at daylight but we were not dissuaded and headed out looking for deer. About 10AM we decided that the deer were both holed up, and smarter than we were, so we headed back to camp. While we were eating lunch and standing around the campfire, a blinding flash of lightning and associated boom of thunder announced the arrival of a real gully washer.

As the rain increased dramatically we heard an approaching rumbling and then a roaring noise coming from the creek we had crossed. Upon inspection saw a surge of water come out of the canyon. Within a few minutes the creek had gained about three feet. The road next to it was eroding fast so we tried rolling a three foot diameter boulder into the water to create a dam. The torrent took it downstream never to be seen again. Once the storm let up a little we scouted the damage. For about a mile downstream the road was washed away and impassable.

When we were about fourteen years old we went through the "survival" stage. One of us found a book that showed how to make snares, deadfalls, and live off the land. We practiced our traps and I think eventually ended up catching a squirrel and the neighbor's dog. We learned to build shelters out of trees and four different ways to start a fire. We could only "hope" that someday we would be so lucky as to be stranded and have the opportunity to prove ourselves.

That day had finally come—we were stranded. The problem was that we were now older and had moved on to other interests (cars and girls). We had plenty of food, firewood, and could probably walk to a phone in about three hours if we really wanted to. It would be a couple of days before the county could get the road passable, so we focused on hunting while being stranded. I can, and have, got through many miserable, wet, and cold nights, but what separates the men from the boys is climbing in a wet sleeping bag that second night.

The spot we liked to hunt was a mile uphill from where we camped the first year, so the next season we decided to backpack farther in. I was late getting to camp, so all the good sleeping spots were gone. It was so steep I had to find a large tree and sleep on the uphill side so as to not roll down the mountain.

Before the hunt we all went to Bob's Army Navy store to purchase rations. When we were choosing them John Foote walked right over to the "beans and franks" and grabbed several. I couldn't believe it! There was steak and all sorts of mouth-watering selections. I am not sure whether they were originally from WWII, Korea, or possible the Civil War, but once we got to camp it was time to heat them up. My steak was one step from inedible. John knowingly looked at me and commented, "There is no way to damage beans and franks."

The next day John and I found a seep at the bottom of a steep canyon. We built a blind and patiently waited for the deer to come drink at dusk. It was a good plan and several times we watched deer slowly make their way down the mountain only to not quite get in range before darkness made a shot impossible.

One evening as we were watching a group of deer work their way toward us a noise echoed from the bottom of the canyon. We had never seen a deer take this route, but if they kept coming we would have a 20 yard shot. Slowly the deer walked up the trail and into view. There were two bucks and two does. John was left of me so he took the left deer and I took the right. This happened many years before the invention of the Two Shooter, so we both drew and shot at relatively the same time. I saw the arrow go into my deer and John shouted that he hit his also. His went west and mine went east. We trailed them until dark but ran out of blood relatively soon on both.

John picked up the trail early the next morning and I showed up as soon as I could get away from work. John's deer was not hit well and lived to drink another day. He mentioned that he had found mine just off of the main trail while hiking in. As we approached the dead deer I told John that it wasn't mine. When I shot my deer I could have sworn that it was a big two point or even a small three point, but the deer lying before us was a spike. The complication was that this small deer had MY arrow in it. To this day it still amazes me of the strange dance between perception and reality.

CHAPTER 17

GETTING THERE

I, and to a lesser degree, my hunting companions, believed in the timeworn motto that "Getting there is half the fun." Do you remember the exhilarating feeling you once had when on the last day of school the final bell rang? That feeling is still available today, once you have loaded up the truck, kissed your wife goodbye (I once knew a man that said his wife was so ugly that he would rather take her with him than kiss her goodbye), picked up a bag of ice and hit the open road.

Work is forgotten, household responsibilities are forgotten, and, to a lesser extent, good manners and taste are forgotten. The invitation is extended to enter into yet another adventure that will build memories and hopefully bring you home with only minor injuries.

Dirt roads bring their own adventures without you even asking, but while on the pavement you must provide your own entertainment. I am not talking about an in-cab DVD player or any electronics other than maybe a CD of Jeff Foxworthy. A good starting place is debating who loves their wife the most. It usually goes something like this, "you love your wife more," "NO, you love your wife more," etc. This exercise usually concludes with the agreement that this will be the last time that women are talked about, or even thought about, until returning home and creating an excuse for why we are two days late. Women would be upset if they ever found out that we talk much more about gas mileage than about them.

There are a few worthy activities to be engaged in while traveling. Great reverence is paid to the man who can spot the most wild game out of the side window while going 70 miles per hour. Extra credit used to be awarded to the driver since he has to look out the front window. That rule has since been rescinded because he is required to stay awake, which gives him more opportunity to look. Advice from the passengers directed toward the driver is usually timely and appreciated. Some drivers show that appreciation by jokingly responding "Shut up or you can drive." Bets are sometimes placed on how far the truck can go before running out of gas, but eventually the talk degenerates to the telling of deer stories. Nothing is looked forward to more than the opportunity of having a "new" hunter in the cab and telling him the same old stories.

Eventually the pavement ends and the fun begins. There is not a more manly feeling in the world than climbing out of the cab, walking to the front of the truck and locking in the hubs. Who ever invented the automatic locking hub should be banished to a small European country and forced to drive a lime green Geo Metro until the day he dies. He has cheated a whole generation out of a reinforcing rite of manhood. The world is fast losing males who wear LEVI'S.

Upon leaving the hard surface, a wise man would have first listened to the weather forecast, inquired about travel restrictions, stopped and examined the current soil and moisture conditions, but we usually just pressed on until stuck. There is logical order of vehicle traction enhancement that, if followed, will mitigate the "stuck" issue.

It all starts with the selection of your hunting "rig." My first rig was a 1961 four-door

Mercury Comet. The only traction enhancement available was to have three of my larger friends accompany me. I tolerated their advice and smell if they agreed to be ballast and occasionally push the vehicle. Next, I borrowed dad's Ford two-wheel drive pickup. When buying the truck, he took the next off-road step by ordering it with "posi-traction." This option directed power to the rear tire with the most grip. Dad bragged how he only had to put on one tire chain when going up the slick dugway to feed the cattle in the winter.

I was too young to be intimidated by steep, muddy, or snowy roads. With a two-wheel drive pickup and a shovel we were invincible. We might have been invincible, but occasionally forward progress failed us. The correct order was to first try rocking the truck back and forth by going from first gear to reverse and back again. If still stuck, all passengers were asked to disembark and put their shoulder to the wheel. When this failed to yield the desired results, the "handyman" came out.

The handyman jack weighs about 30 pounds and is about four feet long. It can raise a 7,000 pound truck off the ground far enough to scare you, but has the nasty habit of sliding off the bumper at just the wrong time. Add the fact that the base of it is usually placed on mud, snow, or an incline and a disaster is in the making. If you are lucky enough to get the truck off the ground and the ruts filled in, the step of lowering the jack will make the toughest man start to turn pale. The jack is designed to be lowered one notch, or inch, at a time, but more often than not it skips this slow procedure of its own accord and just slams to the ground. Heaven help the man within ten feet. The man who invented the handyman jack should first be given a medal and then beaten with it.

I used to work with a man who owned an International Scout 4X4. He was a wise man, but considered a little bit of a pansy by our crowd. He would drive in two-wheel drive until he got stuck, put it in four-wheel drive, get unstuck, turn around and head for home. I never thought I was having any fun if I was only in two-wheel drive.

There were few four-wheel drive trucks available when I was young, but a whole new world opened up to me the first time Grandpa Colledge let me ride in his jeep. It was WWII surplus, painted bright yellow and, of course, named "Old Yeller." We once drove up an abandoned road to retrieve a deer, and I still remember how it crawled up the washed out parts with ease. I vowed that someday I would own a vehicle that had both front and rear axles powering me up the mountain.

Someday came about twelve years later when I acquired a 1966 GMC 4X4. It was a railroad surplus truck with a long narrow bed and a V6 that the previous owner had replaced with a Chevy 327 (it overheated). I swapped the narrow bed out for a wide one from Uncle Bert's salvaged 66 Chevy, had Cousin Neal paint it a sickly shade of green, and was ready to conquer the outback.

The GMC was responsible for permanently corrupting me with the desire to go up the mountain when others failed. My brothers would draw straws to see who would utter the words, "bet you can't get there." In most arenas I am not super competitive, but I do acknowledge my weakness in not being able to stop and say "this is far enough."

We were in Colorado and it had been raining all night. The next morning we started up the mountain, but quickly tired of going sideways and driving by looking out the side window. I asked my son Clint, whose truck we were riding in, if he had tire chains. He answered in the affirmative, but much to my surprise, said that he had never put them on before. Tire chain installation school was called to order and once the proper classroom was found (six inches of mud to lie in), instructions began.

There are two basic methods of installing chains. The first is to jack each wheel off the ground and snuggly attach the chain around the tire. This method has the advantage of getting the tension correct but subjects the installer to being maimed by the previously mentioned handyman jack.

An alternative method is to carefully lay out the chain in front of the tire and then slowly drive onto it. The chain is then connected, and driven until it almost falls off and then retightened. A third and seldom used method is to install the chain in a dry comfortable place long before it is needed. No one I know uses this method; they just default to method number one because their vehicle is immobile and offers no alternative.

I was dismayed while reading the manual for my current pansy truck (which has automatic hubs and a knob instead of a lever to engage four wheel drive), to find that they prohibit placing chains on the front tires. Any serious traveler of the unpaved knows that if you only have one set of chains you put them on the front. Placing them on the front is advantageous because steering is improved and the weight of the motor aids in traction. Traction is important, but staying out of the deep ruts and becoming high centered is what gets you places. This can be accomplished in several ways. Finesse and careful attention to wheel placement will help, but I personally subscribe to the theory of installing tires of one size larger diameter than everyone else.

A lesser-known method of going up steep, muddy, rutted hills is what I like to call the "diagonal dance." The term "dance" refers to the nearly out of control truck bouncing side to side, and gyrating up the hill. The front left tire is placed in the right rut while the right front is out of any rut. The truck goes up the hill sideways without high centering. We once watched a jeep (I am a Bronco man so I refuse to capitalize jeep), make several attempts at climbing a muddy rutted hill. Admitting defeat, he turned around and headed down. As he drove past he told me I couldn't make it. The gauntlet was thrown, the diagonal dance commenced, and we laughed at him from atop the hill.

While living on the ranch we had a D4 Cat dozer. I remember it as being monstrous, but in hindsight it was probably only monstrous to an eight year old. It had a blade in the front and a winch on the back. I marveled at the ease with which large logs for the bridge Dad was building were maneuvered with the winch. After the GMC, and a green Ford 4X4, I acquired a 1979 3/4 ton Ford Supercab longbed 4X4 named "Big Red." The boys named it because it was indeed big and red.   With memories of my youth on the ranch I took the next step and purchased a Warn 8274 winch. With the winch installed on Big Red I dared venture into areas and conditions even I had previously (and wisely) avoided. If I got stuck now the only option would be waiting for spring.

While driving the hogs back in Fruitland, we hit a large drift that pushed us over the edge of the road. The options were, 1) roll downhill 300 yards, 2) winch up, or 3) wait for spring. We chose number two. It took several hours and a few tense moments but eventually Big Red was winched up the mountain sideways.

There was twelve inches of new snow, and once we were chained up on all four, we decided to take a new route down the mountain. We lost the road in a large clearing that had drifted over, but we knew we had found the gully that ran alongside of it when the truck flopped on its side. We exited from the uphill doors and proceeded to look for a tree that would accept our winch cable. The nearest one was at least 350' away.

With the 150' of cable on the drum, 150' of spare winch cable, two tow chains, a tow strap, and a jump rope, we reached the tree. Once the cable was secured the winch popped us right out. There were other times the winch either saved us or lulled us into a false sense of security, but most of the winch's life was spent in assisting other vehicles from their own individual predicaments.

We rounded the corner only to find a jeep had parked in the middle of the trail. As we pulled around it a piece of sagebrush pushed the fan into the radiator and ate an unrepairable hole in it. We got every canteen, bottle and container that would hold water, filled them at the spring, and headed three miles to a service station.

With the hood open, one person would stand on the winch bumper and slowly dribble water into the radiator hose that went to the motor, while another stood in the bed to give directions to the driver, which lacked the ability to see through the hood. We made it to the river, refilled the containers and only had to stop and cool off once before reaching the station.

The next couple of hours were spent on a scavenger hunt in the service station's junkyard.

We found an old radiator that still held water but the hose connections were on the exact wrong corners; no problem. With several lengths of hose, a few adapters, some clamps, wire, and a lot of duct tape we fired her up, headed toward the mountain and returned to hunting. About two months later I got around to installing a new radiator.

There is a bend in the road on the north slope of Mount Terrell that we refer to as "Cadillac Corner." One year on the bow hunt it rained all night and the next day. We had Big Red chained up on all four and were coming down the road heading for town to pick up supplies. As we slid around a muddy corner we saw the strangest sight!

A nearly new Cadillac Eldorado was half on and half off the road. "What an idiot" we cried in unison. We have been known to go where we should not have, but this guy was rewriting the book. Vehicles were backed up ten deep in both directions because he had the road totally blocked. We pulled around the trucks ahead of us because we had the only winch. Half an hour later we had him back on the road and turned back downhill.

I asked what possessed him to try this almost impassable road. He said that when he started up the canyon the road was bone dry and as soon as it got muddy he started looking for a place to turn around. When he finally found a suitable spot it was so muddy that he slid off. We didn't really believe him but as we proceeded down the road it got less muddy by the foot and within a quarter of a mile was only damp. The cloud that had been our constant companion for the last two days sat on the top of the mountain but stopped part way down.

I was the oldest boy and had my license first, so I usually drove. Being the driver seemed to stick, and that is OK by me. If we go fishing Larry brings the poles, if we need pictures Gordy or Craig takes them, if we need someone to bring the jerky Grant is in charge. If everyone will fit in one truck I drive. I have enough food, tools, extraction gear, maps and parts on my truck to survive most catastrophes. We might have been a day or two late but we always managed to make it home.

Most men my age will stay home if it even clouds up. I tell myself that I don't intentionally look for challenging situations, but history has proven me wrong. I do not get quite as excited by the thoughts of chaining up as I used to, but if the opportunity to go exploring presents itself, a small smile might appear.

THE DEER HUNTER'S OATH

CHAPTER 18

LYNNE

My dear wife Lynne has always supported me in my hunting escapades. She bought groceries, sewed the boys hunting vests, and always sent enough cookies for the whole camp. Although she went with us a few times and has shot a couple of deer, she is usually content to kick us out of the house and stay up all night doing some activity that she can't do with us home bothering her.

When she was 14 she took the hunters safety class. She was the only girl but when it came time to qualify on the range, she out-shot all of the boys.

The first time I took her with me was in high school. It was cold as we hiked up the canyon in about three inches of snow looking for deer. After going a half mile I glanced down at her feet. She was wearing low top girley tennis shoes. Even though she had not complained I could tell that she was freezing and her toes had to be near falling off. We turned around and headed for the truck. I mentioned that before we went hunting again we should get her some boots. Lynne had hiked Mount Timpanogos (11,752') when she was five years old with her dad, and several times since. She probably had several pairs of hiking boots in her closet but when I later asked about them, she commented that they looked too "clunky" and she wanted to look nice for me.

The first week of every hunt was, of course reserved for the guys, but some years she accompanied me later in the season. For many years I have put Lynne's name in the deer hunt draw, naively assuming that is what she wanted me to do. Last year her luck changed and she drew a Henry's management tag. I thought the luck that "changed" was a good thing. However she informed me that she was not sure she wanted to go. After many discussions in which we talked about me ASS U ME ing things, it was agreed we would take a weekend and scout the Henry's before deciding.

We left home on a Friday afternoon and drove to Hanksville. After eating dinner in town we pointed the truck towards Mount Ellen and started looking for deer. It didn't take long to find several impressive deer, some that would be legal for her to shoot and some that were just incredible to look at. One in particular caught our attention. It was three on one side as required, and had six points, all coming off the main beam on the other side, making it look like a whitetail.

We pitched a tent when it got dark, set up the cots with thick pads, and had a good night's sleep. In the morning we looked at more great deer, went out through Capital Reef, bought lunch and leisurely rode home. I think I found the secret. Her deer hunt needed to look like a *vacation*.

After another scouting trip (vacation) she was actually looking forward to going. I know that she secretly wanted a new gun for this hunt so I wisely got her a single shot Encore in 25-06. We went target shooting several times and I think she can still out-shoot most of the boys. I booked a motel in Hanksville for the week of her hunt, loaded up and we were off.

On opening morning we ate breakfast, loaded the Samurai and drove up the mountain. In the summer we decided that a side by side would be the best way to get around the mountain, but we were not crazy about the dust and cold, so Larry fixed us up with a Suzuki Samurai. It is essentially the same size as a side by side but with doors, radio, and heater.

We didn't find a good deer in the morning but after lunch I spotted two decent bucks about a mile away. They were both legal three points and one was over 30 inches. We drove to within 500 yards and started hiking. Lynne has had a hip replaced and back problems so we were taking our time. When we were close to where we could shoot, a group of four people came up behind us. There were three men and a girl in her twenties, who had the permit. They had seen the deer and like us, were after it. However, they were several decades younger and would surely get in front of us. They stopped before passing us and asked our plans. After hearing that we had seen the deer before them, they graciously asked if they could tag along and watch Lynne shoot it.

As we set up to shoot they mentioned they had been scouting this particular deer for most of the summer. We also learned that this was the girl's first hunt and she was there on an alternate tag. An alternate tag is one where the original person who drew the permit has turned it back. For reasons known only to women, Lynne felt that there were too many coincidences and that the girl should have this deer. "You should shoot it," Lynne said. The girl replied, "No, you shoot it." When men are involved the "who shoots the deer" conversation often happens, but in reverse. The young girl shot the deer which ended up being 31.5 inches wide.

Over the next three days we saw a lot of nice deer but not the three by six that we had seen while scouting. I mentioned the deer to a gentleman we saw on the mountain and he said someone told him it had one of its antlers broken off. Sure enough, that night we found her deer and it was missing the side with six points.

Every day was a new adventure. We saw hundreds of deer and spectacular new country, but no shooters. The last day of the hunt dawned cold and windy. We were the last hunters on the mountain and where we had seen numerous deer the days before, now they were all holding tight. The morning was almost over when we turned a corner and there stood a monster. It was the tallest rack (25") I have seen in over fifty years of hunting. Once it was confirmed that it had four on one side and three on the other Lynne calmly made a perfect shot. As it dropped she uncharacteristically jumped up and down with excitement. (Quite a reaction from someone who was not sure she even wanted to hunt.)

She checked in with the Fish and Game and they said that it was one of the largest management deer taken that year. The horns were mounted and I then asked her where to hang them. (Although she had once let me display my trophies in the house she had long ago declared our home to be animal head free.) Quite to my surprise she said to hang them in the hall where she could see them every time she went downstairs. I heard her talking to my son's wife about decorating the skull with sequins and rhinestones, but I don't foresee doing that to any of mine.

The Henry Mountains are one of my favorite places on earth and this was one of the most memorable hunts (vacations) I have ever been on.

CHAPTER 19

ROVER

In the West it is looked upon with disfavor and, in most cases is illegal to use a dog while hunting deer, but there are very few deer hunters who don't own a dog.   A real hunting dog is a necessary part of a young man's apprenticeship in the art of hunting.   The dog serves as companion, friend, foot warmer, and sometimes even scares up a pheasant. It is said that if you were to accidentally lock your wife and hunting dog in the trunk of your car, and after an hour or so open it up, the dog would be the only one glad to see you.   We all have dog stories and the following is mine.

We got Rover right after we moved to Manila in the summer of 1957. We had been in the house just a short time and I was excited about starting Kindergarten in the fall. I do remember the day we brought him home. I vaguely remember picking him out of the litter, or maybe not. It is interesting to try and go back 50 odd years and differentiate between perception and reality.

About sunset, after things had settled down a bit, I remember sitting with him on my lap in the garage. I think we were both worn out and what I remember is sitting there for the longest time (it might have really been fifteen minutes, but it seemed like an hour) just snuggling. He was probably asleep, but at that moment I was the happiest kid in the world. We had a new home in the country, fields to explore, and pheasants to find.

Rover was my constant companion for about thirteen years. I let the other members of the family borrow **my** dog occasionally, but he was really mine. He was with me on every scouting trip in the neighborhood, ran along my bike on the way to friends' houses, guarded our house at night, collected cockle burs in his long red hair, and was smart enough to stay out of the road (Gordy's subsequent dogs had issues with the road thing).

When we moved to Fruitland he became the Ranch Dog, faithfully executing the responsibilities of keeping the turkeys off Dad's truck, letting us know when a stranger was approaching, and protecting the family from the ever present threat of chipmunks. He especially hated chipmunks. We would hear often him whining and growling at a chipmunk that he had cornered but could not get to.

Rover was also a great goose hunter. When we moved to the ranch there were about two dozen domestic geese that had gone wild and lived near the river. One day I decided that Mom would really appreciate a goose for dinner. With my trusty .22 and Rover along my side we were off to provide for the family. Upon finding the gaggle I dropped one with a well-placed flock shot. About this time Rover figured out that we were goose hunting (I guess I had neglected to inform him of our plans), so instead of merely retrieving the downed bird he went after them himself. A short time later the score was Jeff one, Rover three.

The first order of business upon arriving at the ranch was to teach him how to jump into the back of the truck. I remember Dad taking about 15 minutes trying to teach him how to do it. He was not too willing until he realized that he would be left behind when we went to the Fruitland general store for our ice cream break.

When we went home for longer periods of time he would ride in the back of the truck with us older boys and keep us warm. If you were relying on Rover for warmth you learned to make him get in the river a day before to wash off whatever he had rolled in during the previous two weeks.

In general Rover despised cats, or at best tolerated and ignored them. Gordy, however, had a cat whose name escapes me that took a liking to the big red dog. I remember looking out the sliding doors to where Rover slept on the porch (he was allowed to look in the house but not actually enter it), and seeing the strange site of the cat sleeping on top of Rover to keep warm. It must have been a mutually beneficial relationship because it went on for some time. As I ponder on it I think it was in his later years when he was getting old and soft.

The main reason people gave for owning a hunting dog in our area was to set and point pheasants. In hindsight it seems to be a strange reason since pheasant season was only three days long. We didn't keep Rover around for his pheasant abilities. I don't think anyone ever told Rover that he was an "Irish SETTER." When he was young he was more of the flush-now-and-ask-forgiveness-later type of dog. Like everyone, in his later years he did slow down and realize the satisfaction gained, and less energy expended, by pointing, setting, flushing, and then hope we missed so as to not have to chase down a wounded bird.

I don't remember exactly when he died other than I was away at college. I think the other kids had a small ceremony and buried him in the pasture. When I got home I walked to his grave and reflected for a little while. Although I was a tough guy, a tear fell. He lived a good life and is in dog heaven. There were hundreds of experiences with my best friend that come and go through my memories, but in general he was the friend that was always willing and always there.

Brother Larry's rebuttal:

Everyone knew from day one that Rover was my dog. Mom told us when she was growing up she had an Irish Setter named Fanny, and it was her dog just because it had hair the same color as hers. So, simple deduction would prove that being the only redhead would make Rover my dog. I specifically remember going over with Dad to pick up the pup. I remember looking at Rover's mother and thinking how pretty and shiny she was. I remember there being several puppies and picking Rover from the litter. (At least I think I remember.)

Many of the qualities that I have today I can attribute to Rover:

When sleeping outside almost every night during the summer Rover would lay on the bottom of my sleeping bag. As the night progressed, he would inch his way up the sleeping bag until I was in a little ball in the top 25% of the bag. *This helped prepare me for sleeping with my wife in my little corner of the bed.*

Rover mastered the pheasant hunting technique of point and jump. Rover would often go in the fields hunting birds by himself. No one was with him to flush the birds, so he simply pointed them for about one second and then jumped them. *This hunting technique taught me how to make that quick shot.* I believe this training is what has allowed me to consistently win the family clay pigeon shooting contests on a regular basis.

While dehorning and castrating the cows, Rover was able to get full use out of the parts that we discarded. He honed the fine art of squishing the horn in his teeth and sucking out the good stuff. *He taught me the value of recycling.*

And we must always remember that I saved Rover's life two times:

In the neighborhood there was a big mean yellow dog. I don't remember whose it was, but it was bigger than Rover. I was over by Aunt Lucille's house when Rover got in a big fight with this monster yellow dog. I remember that the dog had Rover by the throat, and I thought that only I could save the day. I started kicking the dog as hard as any six or seven year old could, and when that and punching did not work I grabbed the dog's tail and started pulling. With a bewildered look on its face the yellow monster turned its head and sunk it vicious teeth into my leg, most likely all of the way to the bone. That courageous act (and the fact that Aunt Lucille, hearing the barking and my screaming, came outside and beat the dog with her broom) saved the day.

I proudly limped back home with a seemingly unhurt Rover wagging his tail by my side. Mom was at home to provide a quick triage. I probably lost about a pint of blood, but it didn't require a doctor visit because mom was able to dab the wound with her trusty bottle of Methylate. This, in fact, hurt more than the dog bite. She was, however, pretty upset, not about the dog fight, but about the holes in my new Levi's. (They weren't really Levi's. We had to get the JC Penney brand because they were 25 cents cheaper, and we couldn't wash them for the first 6 months because it made them last longer. I think the reason I walk so funny today is from wearing those stiff imitation Levi's, unwashed for 6 months and tripping over the cuffs because they were always 4 inches too long.)

The second time I saved Rover's life was a little less dramatic. It was on a hot summer day on the ranch in Fruitland. I was sitting in the back of the truck with Rover while dad was doing something with cows by the corral near the river. Rover wasn't looking very good. He was lying in the truck and was very lethargic. I immediately felt his nose and it was dry.

Back in the day, every eight year old boy knew that if a dog's nose got dry it was very sick and was going to die. I was in a quandary as what to do. I was the only one around and I know Rover's time on this earth was very short. I must do something quick or lose my precious companion. I had an idea. I spit on Rover's nose rubbed it around until it was wet all over. Rover immediately felt better, he jumped up, wagged his tail and we were off to play and chase pot guts. And just for the record, I am still upset about the goose hunt with Rover. I was back in Pleasant Grove visiting a friend or cousin during that hunt.

Brother Gordon's rebuttal:

I had a little different recollection of Rover. I do remember him hanging out in the backyard and getting burrs out of his long red hair. He would usually sleep with us kids under the clothesline. Unfortunately, the main thing I remember about Rover is looking out in the backyard one day (I think it may have been a Sunday). Rover was sleeping in the backyard, but unfortunately later on he was still sleeping in the backyard and had not moved. So the main thing I remember about him was seeing him dead on the lawn. This made much more of an impression on a tender lad of eight than the death of any relative possibly could. To this day, whenever I see a pet (or person) sleeping I always keep looking until I see them breathe. My first thought is to assume everything is dead until otherwise confirmed.

So while the older kids have great memories of tromping through the hills with their best friend by their side like the first part of Old

Yeller, my memories will always be like I missed the whole movie and came in for the last five minutes, immediately followed by reading the last chapter of Where The Red Fern Grows.

Brother Grant's Rebuttal:

I believe I remember Rover's last pheasant hunt. We were hunting in Wadley's field next to Lynn Smith's house. Mr. Smith said that he saw several pheasants in the field early in the morning. Several other hunters were in the field (no doubt trespassers). Since we knew the Wadley's we had the right to be there. Other hunters with dogs were ahead of us and we were pretty depressed with our prospects of getting a pheasant.

As we approached the big overgrown ditch in the field, Rover went into the ditch and flushed about 25 pheasants (as from Larry's description I am sure Rover pointed for one second before he flushed the birds, but we couldn't see him in the ditch). With all the other hunters (trespassers) around we only got two birds that flew over toward Smith's field. (As I recall I got one and dad got the other one—but that could be selective memory.) The next morning was

Sunday and we went to church and Rover was sleeping (or, as Gordon pointed out, he wasn't sleeping at all) after his hard day hunting.

CHAPTER 20

HEART ATTACK

When I was 39 years old Dad looked at me one day and solemnly said, "Son, I was your age when I had my first heart attack." He was told at a young age that he had a heart murmur, but at the time there was nothing they could do for it. He ignored the diagnoses and became determined that it would not slow him down. His first heart attack was in 1966 when I was 14. I remember Mom explaining the situation to us kids and trying to make it not sound as serious as it really was, but I was old enough to be scared. I don't think you are ever really ready for your Dad to die. I was in my late forties before I could even imagine living my life without his advice and companionship.

The doctor told Dad that he had to give up working construction for several months, start taking heart medication, and quit smoking. Heart surgery was still a fairly new procedure or he would have been a candidate. He recuperated for a while, but went back to work before he should have.

It was 1982 when Dad, Larry, and I pulled up to the Grassy Knoll to start the deer hunt. Dad wanted to be dropped off and hike to the Big Draw.   Larry and I pulled away and slowly headed to the west. Before we had gone too far we heard a shot from Dad's location.   We backtracked and saw him sitting in the oak brush about 300 yards from where we had left him. Larry hollered, "Was that you who shot"?

"Yes".

"Did you hit him?

"Yes"

"Where is he?"

"In the brush between us but I can't hike that far."

That was strange because Dad had been able to physically do about anything he wanted and was a good hiker. Larry helped him to the truck while I took care of the deer. He didn't look too good so we cut the morning short and took him back to camp.

Later that afternoon he was not doing any better, so we took him home. I hadn't thought about his previous heart attack in ten years, but we later found out that that was exactly what he was experiencing.

The next day he went to the doctor who sent him to the hospital and from there into open heart surgery. As he awoke from a triple bypass operation he whispered to me, "If this happens again just let me die."

I guess heart surgery is similar to childbirth because after his recovery he was in great shape for another ten years and told me to forget about the 'letting me die" comment. Dad lived through many more deer camps and one more heart surgery before exiting this earth.

A couple of my older hunting companions and I have come to a gentlemen's agreement. When the time comes that one of us is so incapacitated that he unintentionally soils himself the others will take him rabbit hunting in the West Desert and forget to bring him home.

When the time comes to leave this earth I can think of no better place than on a hill near deer camp surrounded by my loved ones that will have to pack me out.

EPILOGUE

Deer hunting has been a big part of my life. At one time I kept track of every deer I had shot, which is now probably over fifty. I recorded the location, size and part of the body I hit them. The count has slowed, not due to less days afield, but I find that I get far more satisfaction out of assisting my kids and grandkids in their quests.

I realized that a column missing on the deer spreadsheet was one that listed the people I hunted with. It was not missing because I couldn't remember who they were, but the people that shared the hunt were almost taken for granted. Not taken for granted in a careless way, but just like an old pair of broken-in hunting boots, had become a natural part of the experience.

I don't crave venison as much anymore—just relationships and experiences with those people who accompany me.

Made in the USA
San Bernardino, CA
15 March 2015